NORDSTROM

FLAVORS

NORDSTROM

FLAVORS

An Artful Celebration of Food

MICHAEL NORTHERN

Photographs by Noel Barnhurst

CHRONICLE BOOKS

SAN FRANCISCO

ISBN 978-0-8118-6383-4

Manufactured in China.

Design and typesetting by Gretchen Scoble
Food and prop stylist: George Dolese
Food stylist assistant: Elisabet der Nederlanden

All-Clad is a registered trademark of All-Clad Metalcrafters LLC; Grand Marnier is a registered trademark of Société des Produits Marnier-Lapostolle; Old Bay is a registered trademark of Old Bay Company; Parmigiano-Reggiano is a registered trademark of Consorzio del Formaggio Parmigiano-Reggiano; Tabasco is a registered trademark of Mcilhenny Company; Valrhona is a registered trademark of Valrhona S.A.

10 9 8 7 6 5 4 3 2 1

Published exclusively for Nordstrom, Inc., by Chronicle Books LLC.

Chronicle Books LLC
680 Second Street
San Francisco, California 94107
www.chroniclebooks.com

This book is dedicated
to my grandson,
Elias Michael Klempay,
who is one among many
lights of my life.

Contents

Preface

It is with particular joy that I take time to reflect on the nineteen years I have spent working in the Nordstrom Restaurant Division, and how this book, *Nordstrom Flavors,* embodies the rigorous path of our culinary development during that period.

Before I came to Nordstrom, I spent many years owning and managing restaurants. When I arrived here, I found myself at the center of a wonderful group of people who worked diligently to bring honest, uncomplicated food to our fifty or so dining rooms across the country. At the time, their goal was to turn out traditional sandwiches and salads to keep our hungry shoppers fed. Frankly, they also hoped to keep them in our stores longer than they might have stayed had they needed to go elsewhere for a bite to eat. Elsewhere in the country—and indeed, just beyond our doors—food service was beginning to experience a dramatic change, with many new experiments in both flavor and restaurant design under way. But Nordstrom dining stayed on a narrow path, close to its original concept of serving the basic "shopper's menu."

As a new team, we set out on a mission that some thought was too aggressive. We sparked controversy with both cherished customers and respected store employees. It was a time of great upheaval and self-development, and we found ourselves confronting the question of whether Nordstrom should have restaurants at all. Our team's vision was clear: we wanted to make Nordstrom a destination for memorable dining, not just someplace to eat while shopping. To make this happen, we first developed four individual concepts to satisfy the particular needs of our stores across the country. The next step, which was crucial to making this monumental change work, was to build a team of talented culinary leaders.

Michael Northern was the first appointment I made. The year was 1996, and his mission, from that day to today, has been to learn and teach the discovery of memorable flavors. Under his culinary leadership, the metamorphosis from simple dining rooms to dining destinations began to gain momentum. Michael and our management team knew that success could only continue if we built a top-tier group of chefs to answer the bell of opportunity.

The wonderful environment of creativity that has resulted has attracted some of the country's best chefs to Nordstrom. All of them that contributed to this book have a similar story: They have learned how to excel at both learning and teaching. As students, they share what they learn about food with one another. At the same time, they act as mentors to the talented teams of culinary professionals that fill our kitchens from coast to coast.

This book, the third cookbook in our portfolio of published stories, serves as a record of this incredible journey—a journey that continues every day in our stores across the country. It is a collection of recipes that promises to bring delicious, unforgettable flavors to your table. My hope is that you will enjoy making these exceptional dishes in your own kitchen, and that you will take pleasure in knowing that many of them are also served in Nordstrom's dining rooms around the country.

Bon appétit!

—John Clem
Vice President
Nordstrom Restaurant Division

Introduction

These are the flavors that we come back to time and again. . . .

Just before sitting down to write those words, I took a short walk down the street to Pike Place Market here in Seattle. A visit to the market always clears my mind and nourishes my soul.

This wonderful market figured prominently in my decision to relocate from the Midwest to the Pacific Northwest. As a chef, I am attracted to it as a moth to flame. More than anywhere else I have been, I feel a deep connection to the food sold at this century-old establishment, a unique institution that grew out of the public's discontent with food prices charged by middlemen and grocers. The market remains a vital, thriving community in which food plays the central role.

Around every corner of this extraordinary place you find inspiring displays of the freshest produce marketed with informative—and sometimes whimsical—signs. At one stall, you might see eye-catching examples of specially selected Pacific Northwest seafood, some of it flying through the air as the fishmongers toss whole salmon back and forth to one another. Travel farther into the market and you will discover a mosaic of small produce stands featuring locally grown farm-fresh fruits, vegetables, and flowers, all of them set out in colorful, cheerful arrangements. The entire setting is further animated by farmers unloading their trucks, tourists exploring the market, and locals gathering in conversational knots around various hot spots. In short, for a chef who lives a life surrounded by food and people in motion, this is a place to feel comfortable—a little slice of heaven that celebrates the belief that it is good to be different, to be distinctive.

It was at Pike Place Market that I first came on the idea that has since grown into this book. The initial thought was simple enough: to provide Nordstrom's talented chefs a place to show off their art in the same manner that the enticing ingredients are displayed at the market. Any chef worth his or her mettle creates a menu based on what ingredients are at their best at that moment in time. Their knowledge of what flavors their clients enjoy the most also comes into play. When a chef walks through the market and sees a mound of freshly foraged chanterelles or a bushel of juicy pears, he or she immediately starts thinking about delicious ways to cook them. A chef's sense memory of a food's flavor instantly kicks in and a recipe is on its way to being created.

In *Nordstrom Flavors: An Artful Celebration of Food,* we feature the tastes that we know our diners love. Our list of favorite flavors doesn't have much to do with the standard quintet of sweet, sour, bitter, salty, and umami. (The last one, umami, is relatively new to the list and is difficult to describe. Most cooks feel it is a flavor enhancer, rather than an actual flavor. For example, mushrooms and soy sauce fall into the umami category.) Our "most valuable players" roster includes zesty fresh herbs; briny, utterly pristine seafood; the dessert stalwarts of chocolate and vanilla; ripe, sweet fruit, especially berries; sizzling grilled food redolent of smoke; eye-opening chiles and other forthright spices; the essential seasonings, salt and pepper; heady garlic, especially when roasted to mellow its flavor; and comforting, flavor-packed slow-cooked foods.

This meant that the book chapters could not follow the traditional breakdown of appetizers to desserts. Instead, it had to be organized by ingredients and flavors. I presented these chapter subjects to Nordstrom's chefs, certain it would woo them into strutting their best stuff. And, as you will see, it did.

All of the recipes were written by Nordstrom chefs from our restaurants around the country. While some of the contributors no longer don their crisp chef whites every day because they now hold executive positions in the restaurant division, each ran kitchens as a chef earlier in his or her career. Because these recipes were written by seasoned chefs, some of them are slightly more challenging than those that appeared in our previous two cookbooks, *Nordstrom Friends and Family* and *Nordstrom Entertaining at Home.* Nevertheless, our team worked hard to tailor them for the home cook, testing and retesting to make sure they were approachable in content, not too challenging in technique, and not insistent on unusual ingredients or hard-to-find equipment.

The chefs I know compare themselves to their peers not just by how well they cook, but also by their skills as shoppers and foragers. For a chef, shopping well is an art form, a passion, a sport, and a competitive marketing advantage. Finding the very best ingredients takes time and discipline. Chefs must understand how to work with their purveyors, especially when it comes to purchasing. As with all cooking, the success of these recipes depends on good ingredients, so buy from specialized and knowledgeable merchants. Shopping like a chef is one giant step closer to cooking like one.

If you shop like a chef, your shopping excursions can become educational. Always ask merchants questions: Why does this particular salmon cost twice as much as the one alongside it? How long will this be in season? Where exactly did this come from? Are there any special ways to cook this? The goal is to establish relationships with merchants who are as passionate about food and food quality as you are. Try to shorten the distance from the farm, land, or sea to your table. The freshness and vibrancy of what you select has a greater direct bearing on your results than the recipe itself does. It makes more sense to buy carrots directly from the farmer with dirt under his or her fingernails than it does to buy a bag of perfectly scrubbed carrots that arrived at some point in the past from who knows where. Even the best cook cannot capture the flavors that are lost in a long transit from farm to table.

The *Nordstrom Flavors* cookbook fights the trend toward the homogenization of our food supply, which is becoming more and more common in some areas. Many chefs know, or at least sense, that this is happening. These recipes hope to overcome such obstacles with the desire to produce real and heartfelt meals with memorable flavors.

No exceptional dish was ever prepared and served with anything less than the most exceptional ingredients. If you desire to be an above-average cook (and if you own this book, I assume that you do), you need to be an above-average shopper. Use all of your senses as you select your food, and you will never have to struggle in the kitchen. Instead, great flavor will come naturally.

These are the flavors that the Nordstrom chefs hope you will come back to time and again. . . .

HERB GARDEN

DILLED GAZPACHO WITH JUMBO LUMP CRAB **19**

SUMMER TOMATO SALAD WITH BASIL PESTO **20**

HERB GARDEN RISOTTO **21**

GOAT CHEESE AND LEEK TART WITH FRESH HERB SALAD **23**

BITTER GREENS AND BLUE CHEESE SALAD WITH ORANGE WALNUT VINAIGRETTE **25**

THYME-SCENTED ROAST CHICKEN **26**

CORN AND TOMATO GRATIN **29**

ZUCCHINI FRITES WITH LEMON AND SAGE **30**

ZUCCHINI AND SWEET POTATO LATKES WITH CHIVE CRÈME FRAÎCHE **32**

ORZO SALAD WITH BASIL AND PARSLEY **33**

CHICKEN PAILLARD WITH ARUGULA SALAD **34**

DIJON HERB-CRUSTED SALMON **37**

DILLED GAZPACHO WITH JUMBO LUMP CRAB

While living briefly on the coast of Spain, I grew fond of this chilled delicacy, probably the most popular of all cold soups. In this version, I add some personal (and very American) touches, such as fresh dill and sweet crabmeat. Of course, gazpacho is traditionally made with fresh ripe tomatoes, but because even in Spain the tomato season is fleeting, some of the best Spanish cooks make the soup with canned tomatoes and tomato juice, and this recipe takes their lead. Enjoy this soup with plenty of crusty bread, preferably while sitting on a beach in the Mediterranean sun! [CHEF MICHAEL LYLE]

Serves 6

3 cups canned tomato juice

1 can (14½ ounces) petite diced tomatoes in juice

⅓ cup plus 1 tablespoon extra-virgin olive oil

2 tablespoons fresh lemon juice

1 tablespoon tomato paste

1 small red onion, finely chopped (1 cup)

1 green bell pepper, seeded, deribbed, and cut into ¼-inch dice (¾ cup)

2 Kirby cucumbers, halved lengthwise, seeded, and cut into ¼-inch dice (1 cup)

1 large ripe tomato, cored, halved, seeded, and cut into ¼-inch dice (1 cup)

2 cloves garlic, minced

1 tablespoon chopped fresh thyme

Kosher salt

Freshly ground black pepper

1 tablespoon coarsely chopped fresh dill

2 tablespoons red wine vinegar

½ teaspoon Tabasco sauce

½ pound jumbo lump crabmeat, picked over for shell bits

At least 12 hours before serving, in a large bowl, combine the tomato juice, canned tomatoes and their juice, oil, lemon juice, and tomato paste. Whisk to dissolve the tomato paste. Stir in the onion, bell pepper, cucumbers, fresh tomato, garlic, and thyme. Season to taste with salt and pepper. Cover tightly with plastic wrap and refrigerate for at least 12 hours or up to 24 hours to develop the flavors.

Just before serving, stir in the dill, vinegar, and Tabasco, and then taste and adjust the seasoning generously with salt and pepper. Ladle the soup into 6 chilled bowls and top with the crabmeat, dividing it evenly. Serve immediately.

CHEF'S NOTE: *Nothing ruins a crab dish more quickly than biting into an errant bit of crab shell. To avoid that, use your fingers to sort through the crabmeat and remove any stray shell bits. During your search, break up the crabmeat into pieces that will fit easily in a soup spoon. Pasteurized crabmeat is readily available from coast to coast and is a reliable product. However, when you find fresh crabmeat, be it West Coast Dungeness or East Coast blue, use it.*

SUMMER TOMATO SALAD WITH BASIL PESTO

When fresh ripe tomatoes are at their peak, they really don't need any embellishment.
A sprinkle of salt and pepper is enough. The next best option is to add milky mozzarella, heady basil,
and mellow olive oil to make a classic *caprese* salad, a signature dish of the Italian island of Capri. Some versions
use basil leaves, but here pesto ensures that every bite bursts with herb-infused flavor. Colorful heirloom tomatoes
offer a double treat of fabulous flavor and dramatic presentation. [CHEF JONATHAN ROHLAND]

Serves 6

BASIL PESTO

½ cup extra-virgin olive oil

⅓ cup freshly grated Parmesan cheese, preferably Parmigiano-Reggiano

2 tablespoons pine nuts, toasted (see Chef's Note)

1 clove garlic, minced

3 cups firmly packed fresh basil leaves

Kosher salt

Freshly ground black pepper

SALAD

½ pound fresh mozzarella cheese, drained and sliced ¼ inch thick

¼ cup Basil Pesto

2 tablespoons balsamic vinegar, preferably a high-quality aged vinegar

3 tablespoons extra-virgin olive oil

Kosher salt

Freshly ground black pepper

4 large heirloom tomatoes (about 2½ pounds), preferably a mixture of colors, cored and sliced into thick wedges

2 tablespoons pine nuts, toasted (see Chef's Note)

8 fresh basil leaves, cut into fine ribbons

To make the Basil Pesto, in a food processor fitted with the metal chopping blade, combine the oil, Parmesan, pine nuts, and garlic. Top with the basil. Pulse until the basil is finely chopped. Then, run the processor, stopping to scrape down the sides of the bowl as needed with a rubber spatula, until the mixture is a coarse purée. Season to taste with salt and pepper. You should have about 2 cups. Set aside ¼ cup to use for this recipe. Transfer the remainder to a covered container (see Chef's Note).

To prepare the salad, arrange the mozzarella slices, overlapping them, around the perimeter of a serving platter. In a bowl, whisk together the ¼ cup pesto with the vinegar and oil to make a vinaigrette. Season to taste with salt and pepper. Toss the tomato wedges in the vinaigrette, and arrange on the platter. Cover loosely with plastic wrap and let stand for up to 30 minutes before serving.

Season the salad with salt and pepper, and sprinkle with the pine nuts and basil. Serve immediately.

CHEF'S NOTE: *Toasting pine nuts releases their oils, giving them an even richer flavor and crispier texture. To toast the nuts, heat a small skillet over medium heat. When it is hot, add the nuts and toast, stirring often, until golden brown, 1 to 2 minutes. Pour the nuts onto a plate and let cool.*

The leftover pesto can be stored for another use. Transfer it a small container, pour a thin layer of oil over the surface (to prevent discoloration), cover tightly, and refrigerate for up to 1 week or freeze for up to 3 months. Bring to room temperature and stir well before using.

HERB GARDEN RISOTTO

One of the best birthday gifts I ever received was the herb garden given to me by my kids. For the dedicated cook, nothing beats having herbs ready to clip and bring fresh flavor to your cooking. This dish is light but earthy, and the lemon complements the herbs with its slightly sharp aroma and taste. Accompany the risotto with a substantial vegetable salad, and sit back and await the compliments from your dinner guests. [CHEF ROB GIBBS]

Serves 4 as a main course or 6 as a first course

1 can (49 ounces) low-sodium chicken broth

4 tablespoons (½ stick) unsalted butter

½ yellow onion, finely chopped

1 shallot, finely chopped

2 cups medium-grain Italian rice such as Arborio, Vialone Nano, or Carnaroli

1½ cups dry white wine such as Pinot Grigio

¾ cup freshly grated Parmesan cheese, preferably Parmigiano-Reggiano, plus more for garnish

2 tablespoons chopped fresh basil

1½ teaspoons chopped fresh oregano

1½ teaspoons chopped fresh thyme

1 teaspoon chopped fresh tarragon

2 tablespoons fresh lemon juice

Kosher salt

Freshly ground black pepper

1 lemon, cut into wedges, for serving

Bring the broth just to a simmer in a saucepan. Reduce the heat to very low to keep the broth hot.

In a deep, wide saucepan or Dutch oven over medium heat, melt 3 tablespoons of the butter. Add the onion and shallot and cook, stirring occasionally, until they are translucent, about 3 minutes. Add the rice and stir until the rice kernels are covered with the butter and the rice feels heavy in the spoon (do not toast the rice), about 2 minutes. Add the wine and cook, stirring constantly, until the wine has almost evaporated.

Add ½ cup of the hot broth to the rice and cook, stirring frequently, until the rice has almost completely absorbed the liquid. Adjust the heat to medium-low to keep the risotto at a steady slow simmer. Continue adding the broth, ½ cup at a time, stirring until the broth is almost completely absorbed before adding the next addition and leaving ¼ cup broth for the final addition. After about 18 minutes, the rice grains will be creamy, plump, and cooked through but still slightly chewy. If you run out of broth before the risotto reaches this point, use hot water. Stir in the remaining ¼ cup broth, the Parmesan, basil, oregano, thyme, and tarragon. Then stir in the lemon juice and the remaining 1 tablespoon butter. Season to taste with salt and pepper.

Spoon the risotto into warmed shallow bowls. Garnish each serving with a lemon wedge and a sprinkle of Parmesan cheese and serve immediately.

CHEF'S NOTE: *Stirring risotto at the stove with your guests in the kitchen can be relaxing, but there are times when a make-ahead approach is better for entertaining. In those cases, cook the risotto for about 15 minutes, or until it is about three-fourths done. Then spread it in an even layer on a parchment paper—lined rimmed baking sheet, cover with plastic wrap, and let cool. Refrigerate the broth if not continuing within 2 hours. When ready to serve the risotto, reheat the broth, heat 1 tablespoon unsalted butter or olive oil in the risotto pot, add the partially cooked risotto, and pick up where you left off, finishing the risotto with the heated broth.*

GOAT CHEESE AND LEEK TART WITH FRESH HERB SALAD

Some of the finest cheese makers in the United States are in Northern California. Nordstrom's Downtown San Francisco Bistro features local ingredients as much as possible, and this tart was created to celebrate creamy, tangy goat cheese from a nearby producer. One of the nicest things about this tart is the buttery pastry, which is pressed into the pan, rather than rolled out. Don't think of the herb salad as an afterthought. It works in tandem with the tart to create a versatile dish that can be served as a first course or a lunch or brunch main course. [CHEF KIMBERLY HAZARD]

Serves 6 to 8

TART DOUGH

1½ cups all-purpose flour

Pinch of fine sea salt

¾ cup (1½ sticks) unsalted butter, chilled, cut into cubes

3 tablespoons ice water, or as needed

FILLING

½ pound sliced bacon, cut into ½-inch dice (1 cup)

1 tablespoon unsalted butter

3 leeks, white and light green parts only, cut into ½-inch dice (1½ cups)

2 large cloves garlic, chopped

¼ cup low-sodium chicken broth

¼ pound rindless fresh goat cheese, at room temperature

½ cup sour cream, at room temperature

2 large eggs, at room temperature

1 teaspoon chopped fresh thyme

½ teaspoon kosher salt

¼ teaspoon freshly ground black pepper

To make the Tart Dough, in a food processor fitted with the metal chopping blade, combine the flour and salt and pulse a few times to mix. Add the butter and pulse until the mixture resembles coarse bread crumbs. Add the ice water and pulse briefly, just until the dough is moist enough to hold together when pinched between your thumb and forefinger. Add more ice water, 1 teaspoon at a time, if needed. Transfer the dough to a clean work surface and gather into a ball. Flatten into a thick disk and wrap in plastic wrap. Refrigerate for at least 30 minutes or up to 1 hour.

Place the dough in a 9-inch tart pan with a removable bottom. Using your fingertips, gently press the dough over the bottom and up the sides, forming a slightly thicker layer on the sides. Freeze for 30 minutes. Meanwhile, position 1 oven rack in the upper third and a second rack in the lower third of the oven and preheat the oven to 400°F.

Line the tart shell with aluminum foil and fill with aluminum pie weights or dried beans. Bake in the bottom third of the oven until the dough looks set, about 10 minutes. Remove the pie weights and foil and reduce the oven temperature to 350°F. Continue baking the tart shell until the pastry is light golden brown, 15 to 20 minutes. If the pastry bubbles, pierce the bubbles with a fork. Transfer to a wire rack to cool.

Meanwhile, make the Filling. In a skillet over medium-high heat, cook the bacon, stirring occasionally, until crisp, about 7 minutes. Using a slotted spoon, transfer to paper towels to drain. Pour out all but 1 tablespoon of the bacon fat from the pan, add the butter, and return the pan to medium heat. Add the leeks and garlic and cook, stirring constantly, until the leeks soften, about 8 minutes. Stir in the broth. Reduce the heat to low, cover, and simmer until the leeks are stewed and tender, about 8 minutes more. Uncover, increase the heat to high, and cook, stirring often, until the broth has completely evaporated, about 4 minutes. Set aside to cool slightly.

continued >

HERB SALAD

½ cup firmly packed small fresh
    basil leaves (or torn large leaves)

¼ cup firmly packed fresh flat-leaf
    parsley leaves

¼ cup cut-up fresh chives
    (1-inch lengths)

¼ cup firmly packed baby arugula
    leaves

¼ cup fresh chervil leaves (optional)

2 tablespoons fresh tarragon leaves

Grated zest of 1 lemon

1 tablespoon fresh lemon juice

¼ cup extra-virgin olive oil

Kosher salt

Freshly ground black pepper

Balsamic vinegar, preferably a
    high-quality aged vinegar,
    for garnish

In a bowl, mash together the goat cheese and sour cream with a fork. Add the eggs, thyme, salt, and pepper and whisk until smooth. Stir in the leeks and the cooled bacon. Carefully pour the mixture into the tart shell.

Bake the tart in the upper third of the oven until the filling is gently puffed and lightly browned and a wooden toothpick inserted in the center comes out clean, about 30 minutes. Let cool on a wire rack for 10 minutes, then remove the pan sides and return the tart on the pan base to the rack.

To make the Herb Salad, in a large bowl, toss together the basil, parsley, chives, arugula, chervil (if using), and tarragon. Sprinkle with the lemon zest and juice, drizzle with the oil, season with the salt and pepper, and toss again.

The tart can be served warm or at room temperature. Cut it into wedges and place on dinner plates. Arrange a mound of the herb salad next to each tart wedge. Drizzle balsamic vinegar over each wedge and serve immediately.

CHEF'S NOTE: *If you have an artisanal aged balsamic vinegar on your shelf, use it for the garnish. Because of its complex flavor and viscous body, it works better as a garnish than the thin supermarket balsamic vinegar.*

BITTER GREENS AND BLUE CHEESE SALAD WITH ORANGE WALNUT VINAIGRETTE

Radicchio, endive, and arugula can be delicious additions to green salads. However, a salad made of only bitter greens can sometimes be too much of a good thing. With lots of experimentation, I discovered that a walnut and orange dressing takes the sharp edge off of the greens, and salty blue cheese helps to balance the flavors. The result is a salad that looks terrific and tastes great. [CHEF RICHARD SILVA]

Serves 4

ORANGE WALNUT VINAIGRETTE

1 cup (4 ounces) walnut halves or
   pieces

3 tablespoons fresh orange juice

2 tablespoons rice vinegar

⅓ cup walnut oil

2 tablespoons extra-virgin olive oil

Kosher salt

Freshly ground black pepper

2 teaspoons chopped fresh chervil

1 head Belgian endive

½ pound arugula, tough stems
   removed

½ head radicchio, cored and cut
   into narrow ribbons

6 ounces blue cheese, preferably
   Maytag, crumbled

Freshly ground black pepper

To make the Orange Walnut Vinaigrette, preheat the oven to 350°F. Spread the walnuts on a rimmed baking sheet and toast, stirring occasionally, until they are fragrant and have darkened, about 10 minutes.

Meanwhile, in a small bowl, combine the orange juice and vinegar. Whisk in the walnut and olive oils. Season with the salt and pepper. When the nuts are ready, remove them from the oven and immediately add them to the vinaigrette. Let stand for at least 10 minutes or up to 2 hours. Stir in the chervil.

To make the salad, remove 12 large spears from the endive and place in a large bowl. Reserve the remainder of the head for another use. Add the arugula and radicchio and toss to mix. Add half of the blue cheese and the walnuts with the vinaigrette and toss again.

To assemble the salad, remove the endive spears from the bowl and arrange them around the perimeter of a large serving platter. Mound the arugula, radicchio, and walnut mixture in the center, and sprinkle with the remaining blue cheese. Grind a few turns of pepper over the salad and serve immediately.

CHEF'S NOTE: *For the deepest nut flavor, be sure the walnut oil is made from toasted walnuts. Most imported walnut oils are produced in this style, and come in cans or dark glass bottles. Domestic oils are often cold-pressed or expelled and not as tasty. Once opened, store walnut oil in the refrigerator, and then let stand at room temperature for about 1 hour before using.*

THYME-SCENTED ROAST CHICKEN

We have this roast chicken at least once a week at my house. It is my family's ultimate comfort food,
plus it comes with a bonus: it is easy to make so you have extra time for enjoying one another's company.
The secret is plenty of thyme, which infuses the meat and juices with herbaceous flavor. I prefer citrusy lemon thyme,
but any kind of thyme will do. When it comes to side dishes, keep it simple: roast some vegetables on another
oven rack, and make a big bowl of mashed potatoes. [MICHAEL THOMS]

Serves 4

Vegetable oil for preparing the
roasting rack

1 bunch fresh thyme, preferably
lemon thyme (about 25 sprigs)

10 cloves garlic

1 whole chicken (about 4½ pounds),
trimmed of excess fat, preferably
organic

2 teaspoons kosher salt

1 teaspoon freshly ground black
pepper

1 lemon, quartered lengthwise

2 tablespoons extra-virgin olive oil

Preheat the oven to 375°F. Oil a roasting rack and place it in a roasting pan.

Chop enough thyme leaves to measure 1 tablespoon; reserve the stripped stems and the remaining sprigs. Mince 3 garlic cloves. Cut each of the remaining 7 garlic cloves in half.

Season the cavity of the chicken with 1 teaspoon of the salt and ½ teaspoon of the pepper. Stuff the cavity with the reserved thyme stems and sprigs, the garlic halves, and the lemon quarters.

In a small bowl, stir together the oil, the remaining 1 teaspoon salt and ½ teaspoon pepper, the chopped thyme, and the minced garlic. Spread the oil mixture evenly over the outside of the chicken. Place the chicken, breast side down, on the prepared rack in the roasting pan.

Roast the chicken for 30 minutes. Turn the chicken breast side up, and reduce the oven temperature to 350°F. Continue roasting until an instant-read thermometer inserted in the thickest part of a thigh without touching bone reads 170°F, about 1 hour and 10 minutes more.

Remove the chicken from the oven and let rest for 5 to 10 minutes. Carve into serving pieces and serve immediately.

CHEF'S NOTE: *When preparing herbs, keep two important tips in mind. First, make sure the herbs are perfectly clean and completely dry. A salad spinner does the best job. Second, use a sharp knife for chopping. A food processor can sometimes mash the herbs, rather than cut them cleanly. Also, when cutting herbs for a garnish, a knife creates a finer mince, which is easier to sprinkle.*

CORN AND TOMATO GRATIN

This dish exemplifies summer freshness: sweet corn kernels just off the cob; plump, juicy tomatoes at the peak of ripeness; and fresh aromatic herbs. Served family style directly from the baking dish, it goes well with just about any grilled meat, poultry, or seafood that comes off your grill. But it also makes a nice vegetarian main course. [CHEF ALYSSA KASPAREK]

Serves 6 to 8

6 red or yellow tomatoes (about 2 pounds), preferably heirloom, cored and cut crosswise into ½-inch-thick slices

Kosher salt

Freshly ground black pepper

3 cups fresh corn kernels (from 4 to 6 ears)

1 cup whole milk

½ cup heavy (whipping) cream

1 fresh rosemary sprig

½ cup mascarpone cheese, at room temperature

2 cups fresh bread crumbs, made from day-old crusty bread

¾ cup freshly grated Parmesan cheese, preferably Parmigiano-Reggiano

½ cup chopped fresh basil

3 tablespoons finely chopped fresh chives

½ cup (1 stick) unsalted butter, cut into small pieces

½ cup freshly grated Romano cheese, preferably *pecorino romano*

Place a large wire rack on a rimmed baking sheet. Arrange the tomato slices in a single layer on the rack and season with salt and pepper. Turn the tomatoes over, seasoned sides down. Let stand to drain off excess juices, about 35 minutes.

Meanwhile, combine the corn, milk, cream, and 1 teaspoon salt in a heavy-bottomed saucepan over medium-high heat and bring to a gentle simmer, stirring often and taking care the liquid doesn't boil over. Reduce the heat to low, add the rosemary, cover partially, and simmer until the corn is tender, about 8 minutes. Remove from the heat, uncover, and remove and discard the rosemary. Let cool slightly, about 10 minutes, and then whisk in the mascarpone until thoroughly combined.

Position a rack in the upper third of the oven and preheat to 375°F. Butter a shallow 9-by-13-by-2-inch baking dish.

In a bowl, stir together the bread crumbs, Parmesan, basil, and chives and season with salt and pepper. Arrange a single layer of tomatoes on the bottom of the prepared baking dish. Sprinkle with one-third of the bread-crumb mixture, then dot with one-third of the butter. Pour half of the corn mixture over the top. Top with half of the remaining tomatoes, bread crumbs, and butter, and then the remaining corn mixture. Top with a final layer of tomatoes and bread crumbs. Sprinkle with the Romano, and then dot with the remaining butter.

Bake, uncovered, until the gratin is bubbling throughout and the top is golden brown, 35 to 40 minutes. Let cool for about 15 minutes before serving.

CHEF'S NOTE: *Fresh bread crumbs are a must to give the gratin the proper crusty topping, so don't be tempted to use sandy commercial bread crumbs. Day-old rustic-style bread, torn into chunks and processed into coarse crumbs in a food processor fitted with the metal chopping blade, works best. If your bread is not day old, spread the crumbs on a rimmed baking sheet and bake in a preheated 350°F oven until the edges are dried out but not toasted, about 4 minutes. Let cool completely before using.*

ZUCCHINI FRITES WITH LEMON AND SAGE

There is something of an edible symphony here, and it might be titled Green on Pale Green with an Accent of Yellow. It could also be called Zucchini French Fries. Whatever you might call it, the almost-verdant flavor of the zucchini, once the squash is stripped of its seedy and overly moist interior, is nearly perfectly accented by the delicate tempura batter. The crisp frites are brought home by the earthy flavor of fresh sage set against the bright, tart taste of lemon juice. You will need a good amount of oil to keep the frying temperature stable, so a large deep fryer or flat-bottomed wok is the best choice for the pan. The touch of oil added to the tempura batter helps to prevent the frites from absorbing excess oil. [CHEF MICHAEL NORTHERN]

Serves 4 to 6

BATTER

2 cups ice water

2 large egg yolks

2¼ cups all-purpose flour

1 tablespoon cornstarch

Pinch of kosher salt

1 tablespoon canola oil

5 small zucchini

About 6 cups canola oil for deep-frying

All-purpose flour for dusting

Fine sea salt

Freshly ground black pepper

2 lemons, cut into wedges

3 tablespoons minced fresh sage

To make the Batter, in a large bowl, whisk together the ice water and egg yolks. Gradually whisk in the flour and cornstarch and continue to whisk just until the batter is slightly thinner than pancake batter. A few lumps should be visible. Add the salt and stir in the oil. Set aside.

Trim off the ends of the zucchini, and then cut each zucchini in half lengthwise. Scoop out the seeds with the tip of a spoon. Cut each zucchini half in half crosswise, and then quarter each section lengthwise.

To make the tempura zucchini, pour the oil to a depth of at least 3 inches into a large deep fryer or flat-bottomed wok over medium-high heat and heat to 375°F on a deep-frying thermometer. Line a large baking sheet with paper towels.

While the oil is heating, place some of the zucchini pieces in a large bowl. Dust and toss them lightly with the flour, shaking off the excess flour. Working with a handful at a time, and using your fingers, dip the zucchini pieces into the batter, lift them out, and then carefully add them to the hot oil. Fry the zucchini, turning them occasionally with a chopstick or wooden spoon, until they rise to the surface and are crisp and a little more than lightly browned, about 3 minutes. Using a slotted spoon or a wire skimmer, transfer the zucchini to the towel-lined baking sheet to drain briefly, and sprinkle lightly with salt and pepper.

Transfer the zucchini to a bowl, squeeze some lemon juice over them, and sprinkle with a little of the sage. Toss gently to combine and serve immediately. Repeat with the remaining zucchini, lemon, and sage, serving each batch as soon as it is ready.

CHEF'S NOTE: *These zucchini frites are best served right out of the oil, so you might want to save this recipe for cooking with friends in the kitchen. If necessary, keep the zucchini warm on a baking sheet in a preheated 200°F oven. To make sure the seasoning adheres well, season the frites—in fact, all fried foods—as soon as they are removed from the oil.*

ZUCCHINI AND SWEET POTATO LATKES WITH CHIVE CRÈME FRAÎCHE

Latkes are often reserved only for Hanukkah, which is unfair to these savory potato pancakes. By incorporating sweet potatoes and zucchini in the traditional recipe, additional color, flavor, and eye appeal come into play. Everyone at the table will be commenting on this unique—and delicious—adaptation. [CHEF KIMBERLY HAZARD]

Makes 16 latkes; serves 4

CHIVE CRÈME FRAÎCHE

1 cup crème fraîche or sour cream

2 tablespoons finely chopped fresh chives

1 teaspoon fresh lemon juice

Pinch of kosher salt

LATKES

1 large sweet potato (1 pound), peeled

1 large Idaho potato (14 ounces), peeled

1 large zucchini (10 ounces), ends trimmed

1 yellow onion

¼ cup all-purpose flour

2 large eggs, beaten

¼ teaspoon baking powder

2 teaspoons kosher salt

½ teaspoon freshly ground black pepper

About 1 cup canola oil for shallow frying

To make the Chive Crème Fraîche, in a small bowl, stir together the crème fraîche, chives, lemon juice, and salt. Let stand at room temperature while you make the latkes.

To make the Latkes, preheat the oven to 200°F. Place a large wire rack on a rimmed baking sheet, and place the baking sheet in the oven. Line a second baking sheet with paper towels, and place next to the stove top.

Using a food processor fitted with the large-hole grating blade or the large holes on a box grater, grate the sweet and Idaho potatoes, zucchini, and onion, combining them in a large bowl as they are grated. A handful at a time, wrap the potato mixture in a clean kitchen towel, wring to remove the excess liquid, and place in a second large bowl. Add the flour, eggs, baking powder, salt, and pepper and mix well.

Pour the oil to a depth of ½ inch into a large nonstick skillet and heat over medium-high heat until the oil begins to shimmer. To form each pancake, carefully add ¼ cup of the potato mixture to the oil, and then use the bottom of a heatproof measuring cup to flatten it into a 2½-inch-wide cake. Do not crowd the latkes in the skillet. Cook until the undersides are a rich golden brown, about 3 minutes. Using a slotted spatula, turn and brown the second sides, about 3 minutes more. Using the spatula, transfer the latkes to the towel-lined baking sheet to drain briefly, and then transfer them to the rack-topped baking sheet in the oven to keep warm. Cook the remaining potato mixture in the same way.

Serve the latkes hot, drizzled with the chive crème fraîche.

CHEF'S NOTE: *Crème fraîche is a very mild cultured cream, similar to sour cream. It is increasingly available at supermarkets, but it can also easily be made at home. To make your own, in a bowl, stir together 1 cup heavy (whipping) cream (preferably not ultrapasteurized) and 3 tablespoons buttermilk. Cover tightly with plastic wrap. Let stand at room temperature until thickened, about 24 hours, depending on the temperature of the room. Use immediately, or store in the refrigerator (where it will continue to thicken) for up to 2 weeks.*

ORZO SALAD WITH BASIL AND PARSLEY

This salad, which offers a lighter, Mediterranean-inspired twist on the usual mayonnaise-based salads, is a wonderful accompaniment to any backyard barbecue. It's made with orzo (rice-shaped pasta), but you can use other small shapes if you like. Like all starch-based salads, the flavor can dull on standing, so reserve some dressing (and add a bit more salt and pepper) to refresh the salad just before serving. [CHEF TONY COLABELLI]

Serves 8

DRESSING

1 shallot, quartered lengthwise

¼ cup red wine vinegar

¼ cup brine from Kalamata olives

1 tablespoon Dijon mustard

1 cup extra-virgin olive oil

Kosher salt

1 pound orzo

1 pint cherry or grape tomatoes, cored and halved lengthwise

½ cup peeled, diced carrot (¼-inch dice)

½ cup minced red onion

½ cup diced red bell pepper (¼-inch dice)

½ cup diced yellow bell pepper (¼-inch dice)

½ cup diced celery (¼-inch dice)

½ cup crumbled feta cheese, plus more for garnish

¼ cup chopped Kalamata olives

¼ cup chopped fresh flat-leaf parsley

¼ cup chopped fresh basil, plus 10 leaves, cut into fine ribbons

Kosher salt

Freshly ground black pepper

Lemon wedges for serving

To make the Dressing, in a blender, pulse the shallot until coarsely chopped. Add the vinegar, olive brine, and mustard. With the machine running, add the oil in a thin, steady stream to form an emulsion. Season to taste with the salt. Set aside.

Fill a large pot three-fourths full of lightly salted water and bring to a boil over high heat. Add the orzo, stir well, and cook until al dente, according to the package directions. Drain into a colander, rinse under cold running water, and drain again. Transfer to a large bowl.

Add the tomatoes, carrot, onion, red and yellow bell peppers, celery, feta, olives, parsley, and chopped basil. Drizzle 1 cup of the dressing over the top and toss to coat evenly. Season to taste with salt and pepper. Cover the salad and the remaining dressing and refrigerate until chilled, about 2 hours. (The salad and dressing can be prepared up to 3 hours ahead.)

Just before serving, add the reserved dressing, and taste and adjust the seasoning with salt and pepper. Sprinkle the salad with feta and the basil ribbons. Serve chilled or at room temperature with the lemon wedges.

CHICKEN PAILLARD WITH ARUGULA SALAD

This delightful recipe draws its inspiration from Italian tradition, and its success depends on selecting the finest ingredients. To ensure large, impressive *paillards* (thin chicken scallopini), insist on organic chicken breast halves that weigh at least 10 ounces after the tenderloins have been removed. The larger size will also give you some latitude when cooking the *paillards*. [CHEF MICHAEL NORTHERN]

Serves 4

DIJON BALSAMIC VINAIGRETTE

⅓ cup plus 1 tablespoon balsamic vinegar

2 tablespoons minced red onion

2 tablespoons Dijon mustard

2 tablespoons firmly packed brown sugar

2 tablespoons chopped fresh basil

½ teaspoon fine sea salt

¼ teaspoon freshly ground black pepper

1 cup extra-virgin olive oil

4 organic boneless, skinless chicken breast halves, tenderloin sections removed and reserved for another use (about 10 ounces each)

Extra-virgin olive oil for brushing and cooking

Fine sea salt

Freshly ground black pepper

10 ounces arugula, tough stems removed

4 plum tomatoes, cored, halved, seeded, and cut lengthwise into thin strips

¼ red onion, thinly sliced

2 lemons, halved crosswise

To make the Dijon Balsamic Vinaigrette, in a blender, combine the vinegar, onion, mustard, brown sugar, basil, salt, and pepper and process until thoroughly combined and smooth. With the machine running, add the oil in a thin, steady stream to form an emulsion. Set aside.

Cut four 12-inch squares of parchment paper. Using a thin-bladed, sharp knife, carefully split each chicken breast in half horizontally, cutting to within about ½ inch of the other side. Open 1 breast out flat, like a book, and place between 2 sheets of plastic wrap. Using a flat meat mallet, pound gently, beginning from the center and working out toward the edge, until the breast is about ¼ inch thick and the size of a dinner plate. Remove the top layer of plastic wrap and brush the exposed surface with the oil. Smooth a piece of parchment over the flattened breast, then turn the chicken breast and parchment over. Pull off the other sheet of plastic wrap and again brush the exposed surface with oil. Lift the edge of the parchment and roll up the chicken breast and parchment into a log. Transfer the log to a plate. Repeat with the remaining chicken breasts. Cover the plate with plastic wrap and refrigerate until needed. This step can be completed several hours in advance of cooking.

Preheat the oven to 250°F.

In a large nonstick skillet (or 2 skillets if you have them) over medium heat, add 2 tablespoons oil and swirl to coat the bottom of the pan. Heat until the oil is hot but not smoking. Unroll a chicken breast, parchment facing down, and season the exposed chicken with salt and pepper. Leaving the chicken on the parchment, carefully flip the chicken breast over into the skillet, parchment side up. Cook for about 1 minute, then remove the parchment (the parchment helps the chicken keep its shape). Season the exposed surface with salt and pepper. Cook until the underside is lightly browned, about 1 minute more. Using a wide spatula, flip the chicken over and cook until the other side is lightly browned and the chicken feels barely firm when pressed in the center, about 1 minute more. Transfer to a baking sheet and keep warm in the oven while cooking the other chicken breasts in the same way, adding more oil to the skillet as needed.

continued >

To make the salad, in a large bowl, combine the arugula, tomatoes, and onion. Drizzle with ½ cup of the vinaigrette and toss gently to coat all of the ingredients evenly. Reserve the remaining vinaigrette for another use (see Chef's Note). Season to taste with salt and pepper.

Arrange the chicken breasts on warmed dinner plates and top each portion with an equal amount of the tossed salad. Garnish each plate with a lemon half. Serve immediately.

CHEF'S NOTE: *The Dijon Balsamic Vinaigrette recipe makes more than you need for this dish, but the remaining dressing can be stored in a jar in the refrigerator for up to 1 month. This dressing lends itself to any salad with a Mediterranean profile and shows a particular affinity for tomatoes, basil, and feta cheese.*

DIJON HERB–CRUSTED SALMON

In our restaurants, salmon is the most popular of all the seafood offerings.
This recipe was developed with that in mind and with the desire to have a preparation that would consistently
deliver great taste and flavor. It quickly proved itself reliable and is now featured on menus in many
of our restaurants. [CHEF KIMBERLY HAZARD]

Serves 6

HERB CRUST

**4 green onions, white and light
green parts only, minced**

**¼ cup firmly packed chopped fresh
flat-leaf parsley**

**¼ cup firmly packed chopped
fresh basil**

**1 tablespoon firmly packed chopped
fresh oregano**

**1 tablespoon firmly packed chopped
fresh thyme**

3 large cloves garlic, minced

⅓ cup extra-virgin olive oil

**6 skinless salmon fillets
(6 ounces each)**

Kosher salt

Freshly ground black pepper

2 tablespoons Dijon mustard

Preheat the oven to 450°F. Line a rimmed baking sheet with parchment paper.

To make the Herb Crust, in a small bowl, stir together the green onions, parsley, basil, oregano, thyme, and garlic. Drizzle in the oil and stir to moisten evenly. Set aside.

Season the salmon on both sides with salt and pepper. Place the salmon, skinned side down, on the prepared baking sheet. Using the back of a spoon, evenly spread 1 teaspoon of the mustard over the exposed surface of each fillet. Using a rubber spatula, evenly spread about 2 tablespoons of the herb crust over the mustard coating on each fillet.

Roast until the salmon is barely opaque when flaked with the tip of a knife, about 10 minutes.

Using a thin, flexible metal spatula, transfer the salmon fillets to warmed dinner plates. Serve immediately.

CHEF'S NOTE: *To ensure bright, clean flavors, use only fresh herbs for this recipe. Dried herbs will yield a disappointing dish. Always cut fresh herbs by hand, using a sharp knife. Avoid chopping them in a food processor, which bruises the leaves, producing muddy flavors.*

SALT AND PEPPER

THREE DAY CURED STEAK IN PEPPER CRUST

This steak is seasoned from the inside out, which calls for salting the meat a few days before cooking. How does the technique work? You salt the outside of the meat, the salt forces the natural moisture in the meat to the center of the steak, and then the salted liquid redistributes itself throughout the steak. Add a coating of cracked black pepper before grilling, and you are on your way to a world-class steak. A top sirloin, also known as a shell steak, New York strip steak, or Kansas City steak, is the best choice here. [CHEF TONY COLABELLI]

Serves 4

4 top sirloin steaks (10 ounces each), 1 inch thick and trimmed of excess fat

8 teaspoons fine sea salt

⅓ cup coarsely cracked black peppercorns

Vegetable oil for the grill

To season each steak, sprinkle 1 teaspoon of the salt on each side. Place the steaks in a 1-gallon lock-top plastic bag, squeeze all of the air out of the bag, and seal it. Refrigerate for 3 days.

Spread the peppercorns on a dinner plate. One at a time, place each steak, flat side down, on the peppercorns and press gently so the peppercorns adhere to the underside. Turn the steak over and repeat. Shake off any loose peppercorns. Let the steaks stand at room temperature for 1 hour before grilling

Meanwhile, prepare a hot fire in a charcoal grill, or preheat a gas grill on high (see Chef's Note, page 127).

Lightly oil the cooking grate. Place the steaks on the grill, cover, and grill until the undersides are well browned, about 5 minutes. Using tongs, turn the steaks over, re-cover, and grill until the second sides are well browned and the meat feels only slightly resilient when pressed in the center, or an instant-read thermometer inserted horizontally through the side of a steak into the center reads 130°F for medium-rare, about 5 minutes more, or until done to your liking.

Transfer the steaks to a platter or dinner plates and let rest for 5 minutes before serving.

CHEF'S NOTE: *Sea salt is made from seawater that is evaporated to create fine or coarse salt crystals. Fine sea salt is great for seasoning and other general cooking chores. Coarse sea salt is too large to sprinkle on food (although you can easily add it to boiling water for cooking vegetables and pasta), and must be crushed first. Some cooks do this in a salt grinder, but, unlike pepper, there is no advantage to using freshly ground salt. (The essential oils in peppercorns start to lose their flavor when exposed to air, so pepper should be ground as close to using as possible. Salt has no essential oils, so grinding salt is more of a nicety than a necessity.) When it comes to a flavor comparison between sea salt and kosher salt, it is a personal choice. But when measuring the two, remember that fine sea salt has smaller crystals than kosher salt, so the volume will be different. If you are measuring and exchanging one for the other, use slightly less sea salt than kosher salt (or a bit more kosher salt than sea salt) to compensate for the difference in the crystal size.*

THREE SEASONED SALT RECIPES

As you might imagine, things can get pretty frantic in a professional kitchen. All of this ebb and flow of activity is driven by one common theme: the need to cook efficiently and deliciously. Truly, the art of operating any kitchen, whether home or restaurant, is knowing how to save time without producing a negative impact on the food. In our kitchens, we often grab one of these three seasoning mixtures to give a dish a savory infusion without opening up a lot of spice and herb bottles. They will likely become indispensable in your home, as well. [CHEF MICHAEL NORTHERN]

Each recipe makes about ⅓ cup

CREOLE SEASONING

2 tablespoons kosher salt

1 tablespoon sweet paprika,

2 teaspoons granulated garlic

2 teaspoons onion powder

1 teaspoon cayenne pepper

¾ teaspoon freshly ground black pepper

¾ teaspoon freshly ground white pepper

½ teaspoon dried thyme

½ teaspoon dried oregano

ALL-PURPOSE SEASONING

2 tablespoons fine sea salt

1 tablespoon granulated garlic

1 tablespoon onion powder

1 teaspoon freshly ground black pepper

½ teaspoon sweet paprika

⅛ teaspoon cayenne pepper

SOUTHWESTERN SEASONING

2 tablespoons kosher salt

1 tablespoon granulated garlic

1 tablespoon onion powder

2 teaspoons ground cumin

2 teaspoons chili powder

1 teaspoon sweet paprika

¼ teaspoon cayenne pepper

To make each seasoning, in a bowl, whisk together all of the ingredients. Pass each mixture through a coarse-mesh sieve into another bowl. Transfer the seasonings to airtight containers and store in a cool, dark place for up to 2 months.

CHEF'S NOTE: *The Creole Seasoning can be used for adding a blast of Louisiana flavor to any dish and for making blackened chicken or seafood. Use the All-Purpose Seasoning for steaks, poultry, or vegetables. When you want some Tex-Mex flavor, give your food a sprinkle of the Southwestern Seasoning.*

BLACK PEPPER AND CARAMEL CHICKEN WINGS

I developed this recipe for Nordstrom's newest restaurant concept, Blue Stove. Thick caramel sauce
creates a sweet background for the spicy notes, including one important ingredient: Tellicherry peppercorns.
For the best results, chop fresh chicken wings for this dish, as frozen drumettes give off too much water when roasted,
diluting the mouthwatering glaze. And cook the wings on a wire rack to allow the hot air in the oven to
circulate around them, helping them to crisp. [CHEF MICHAEL NORTHERN]

Serves 6

4 pounds chicken wings

1½ cups homemade or store-bought caramel sauce

⅓ cup soy sauce

3 tablespoons Sriracha chile sauce

1 tablespoon kosher salt

2 tablespoons freshly ground Tellicherry peppercorns

5 cloves garlic, very finely minced

Vegetable-oil cooking spray for preparing the rack

Using a cleaver or a heavy knife, cut each wing at its 3 joints. Set aside the drumettes and second joints for this recipe, and reserve the wing tips for another use (such as making stock) or discard.

In a small bowl, whisk together ¾ cup of the caramel sauce, the soy sauce, chile sauce, salt, peppercorns, and garlic to make a marinade. Place the chicken wings in a lock-top plastic bag and pour the marinade over the wings, coating them evenly. Squeeze all of the air out of the bag and seal it. Refrigerate for at least 12 hours or up to 24 hours, turning the bag occasionally.

Preheat the oven to 375°F. Line a large rimmed baking sheet with aluminum foil. Place a large wire rack on the baking sheet, and spray the rack with cooking spray.

Put the wings in a colander to drain off the excess marinade, and then arrange them on the rack on the baking sheet. Roast until the skin is crispy and deep mahogany and the meat has begun to pull away from the bone, 35–40 minutes. Remove from the oven and transfer the wings to a large bowl.

Drizzle the wings with the remaining ¾ cup caramel sauce and toss. Return to the rack on the baking sheet and bake until the wings are freshly glazed, about 6 minutes.

Transfer the wings to a serving platter, let cool just slightly, and then serve.

CHEF'S NOTE: *Tellicherry peppercorns, named for a town in India, are renowned for their fruity, fragrant bouquet, with a depth of flavor and pungency that no other peppercorns can deliver. They owe their superior reputation in part to the fact that they are usually picked from the top of the vine, where they grow larger than they do on the lower area. Do as we do in our restaurants and grind peppercorns as they are needed, keeping their essential oils locked inside until the last second.*

CHOCOLATE TRUFFLES WITH FLEUR DE SEL

Making your own chocolates sounds more difficult than it is. Just as in the famous *I Love Lucy* episode,
the hard part isn't making the chocolates, it's trying not to eat them in the process. What's unique about these truffles is the
touch of coarse, flaky French sea salt that anoints each one. It gives the truffles an exotic accent that cuts their richness and pushes
them toward becoming the ultimate chocolate indulgence. [CHEF KIMBERLY HAZARD]

Makes about 16 truffles

¼ cup heavy (whipping) cream

8 ounces high-quality semisweet chocolate, coarsely chopped

4 tablespoons (½ stick) unsalted butter, cut into small cubes

¼ teaspoon pure vanilla extract

1 teaspoon *fleur de sel* (see Chef's Note)

¼ cup Dutch-processed cocoa powder

In a saucepan over medium heat, warm the cream just until it begins to simmer. Remove from the heat and add the chocolate and butter. Let stand until the chocolate and butter soften, about 5 minutes. Stir until the mixture has fully melted and is smooth. Let cool for 10 minutes, and then stir in the vanilla.

Scrape the mixture into a shallow dish. Cover with plastic wrap and refrigerate until firm, at least 4 hours or up to 24 hours.

Using a melon baller, scrape and scoop the chocolate mixture, quickly rolling each portion into a ball between your palms. If the truffles start to become soft and messy as you shape them, your hands are too warm. Dip them in ice water, dry them well, and then continue making the truffles. As the truffles are shaped, place them on a baking sheet.

Spread the salt in a small bowl. Put the cocoa in another small bowl. One at a time, dip each truffle into the salt so just a few flakes adhere to a small area on it. Then place the truffle, salt side up, in the cocoa and roll to coat, trying to leave the salted area untouched. Transfer to a plate. Cover loosely with plastic wrap and refrigerate until ready to serve or for up to 5 days.

Let the truffles stand at room temperature for about 15 minutes before serving.

CHEF'S NOTE: Fleur de sel, *literally "sea flower," is a French salt made from evaporated salt-water along the coast of Brittany. As the water evaporates, salt crystals form. If it is a windy day, the crystals quickly sink and mix with the mineral-rich clay soil below, yielding* sel gris, *or "grey salt," another celebrated salt. On calm days, the workers are able to rake off the pale flakes on top, which are* fleur de sel. *As would be expected, this yields a delicate crystal that melts quickly on the tongue and leaves behind a pure salt flavor. Other countries produce sea salt with similarly flaky crystals, such as British Maldon sea salt. Such salts are often called finishing salts because they are sprinkled on dishes just before serving. This allows their full flavor and texture to be savored.*

GRILLED ASPARAGUS WITH LEMON SEA SALT

Grilled asparagus is in vogue, and you would be correct in wondering if anyone simply boils the spears anymore.
But the truth is grilling is a great way to prepare asparagus, and the grill adds its own flavor. It's easy, too, and the asparagus
can be served as an appetizer or a side dish. The lemon-scented sea salt provides the perfect accent. [DAVID KIM]

Serves 4

1 pound not-too-thin asparagus

1 lemon

2 teaspoons flaky sea salt such as *fleur de sel* or Maldon (see Chef's Note, page 44)

2 tablespoons extra-virgin olive oil

Freshly ground black pepper

Prepare a medium-hot fire in a charcoal grill, or preheat a gas grill on medium (see Chef's Note, page 126).

Snap off the woody stem ends from the asparagus. Using a vegetable peeler, peel the stalks to within about 4 inches of the tips.

Grate the zest from the lemon into a small bowl. Add the salt to the zest and rub together with your fingers until combined. Squeeze the juice from the lemon into a separate small bowl.

In a shallow dish, toss the asparagus with the lemon juice, and then with the oil. Place the spears on the grill, arranging them perpendicular to the grid so they don't fall through. Grill until you see marks seared on the undersides of the asparagus, about 2 minutes. Roll the asparagus over and grill until the second sides are seared and the spears are crisp-tender, about 2 minutes more.

Using a spatula, transfer the asparagus to a platter. Sprinkle with the lemon salt and season with pepper. Serve hot or at room temperature.

LEMONGRASS-CURED SALMON

The best recipes are often created out of necessity. My sous-chef, Dan Perrine, and I needed a cured salmon dish for a new menu. We started with the familiar dill, salt, and sugar, and the results, though good, were not as exciting as we wanted. We literally rummaged through the refrigerator to get inspiration, and lemongrass came to the rescue. This is a great dish to have on hand for serving as a first course with toast points and salad, or as a brunch dish with scrambled eggs. [CHEF KEITH BREEDLOVE]

Serves 6 to 8

LEMONGRASS CURING PASTE

¼ cup coriander seeds

2 tablespoons rainbow peppercorns

1 shallot, coarsely chopped

2 stalks lemongrass, tender inner bulb only, thinly sliced

1 cup sugar

1 cup kosher salt

2 tablespoons dark rum

2-pound center-cut salmon fillet, skin and pinbones removed and blood line (the dark flesh line running along the bottom) trimmed away

To make the Lemongrass Curing Paste, preheat the oven to 350°F. In a small baking dish, spread the coriander seeds and peppercorns. Bake until the spices are aromatic, about 8 minutes. Remove from the oven and let cool.

Using a food processor fitted with the metal chopping blade or a blender, combine the shallot and lemongrass and pulse until finely chopped. Add the cooled spices and process until the mixture forms a paste, about 2 minutes.

In a bowl, mix together the sugar and salt. Stir in the lemongrass paste and mix well. Sprinkle with the rum and mix until the mixture is evenly moistened.

To cure the salmon, have ready 2 glass or ceramic baking dishes: one dish large enough to hold the salmon fillet and the other dish slightly smaller so it will rest just inside of the larger dish. Rinse the salmon on both sides under cold running water for 30 seconds, and pat dry with paper towels. Lay a sheet of plastic wrap twice as long as the salmon on a work surface. Place the salmon, skinned side up, on the plastic wrap. Rub the entire top of the salmon with half of the curing paste. Carefully turn the salmon over and rub the second side with the remaining paste. Wrap the salmon in the plastic wrap, and then wrap securely again in a second sheet of plastic wrap. Place the salmon in the larger baking dish and rest the second dish on top. Fill the top dish with a few heavy food cans to weight the salmon evenly. Refrigerate, turning the salmon over every 12 hours, for at least 48 hours or up to 72 hours.

When ready to serve, remove the salmon from the refrigerator, unwrap the salmon, and quickly but thoroughly rinse off the curing paste under cold running water. Pat the salmon dry. Using a very sharp, thin-bladed carving knife held at a slight diagonal, cut the salmon into very thin slices and arrange on a platter. Serve chilled.

CHEF'S NOTE: *Run your fingers along the top of a salmon fillet and you are likely to feel a line of very small bones running its length. These little bones lurk just under the surface and can be inadvertently swallowed, so they must be removed. Pull them out with a pair of small needle-nosed pliers or flat-tipped tweezers, always pulling them the direction they grow, rather than straight up, which can rip the flesh.*

CRACKED PEPPER AND CHIVE SEARED SCALLOPS

I make this incredibly easy dish year-round in my home kitchen. In the summer,
I serve it with a salad of mixed greens and heirloom tomatoes tossed with lemon vinaigrette. In the winter,
I serve it with an asparagus risotto. Either way, the unfussy flavors go well with many other ingredients. If possible, use diver,
or day-boat, scallops, which are harvested and brought to port the same day, rather than scallops that have been
left on a boat for many days, where they are kept "fresh" with preservatives. [MICHAEL THOMS]

Serves 6

2 pounds jumbo sea scallops,
preferably diver

1½ tablespoons coarsely ground
black pepper

Grated zest of 2 large lemons
(1 tablespoon)

1½ teaspoons kosher salt

4 tablespoons extra-virgin olive oil

¼ cup finely chopped fresh chives

Preheat the oven to 375°F. Have ready a shallow baking dish in which the scallops will fit in a single layer.

Separate and discard the tough small muscle from the side of each scallop. Dry the scallops well on paper towels. In a small bowl, mix together the pepper, lemon zest, and salt. Season both flat sides of each scallop with the pepper mixture.

In a large nonstick skillet over high heat, heat 2 tablespoons of the oil until very hot but not smoking. Add half of the scallops, with a flat side down. Cook until golden brown on the undersides, about 1 minute. (Be patient and don't prod and move the scallops; they will brown better if left undisturbed.) Using tongs, turn the scallops and brown on the second sides, about 1 minute more. Transfer to the baking dish. Repeat with the remaining 2 tablespoons oil and the scallops.

Bake the scallops until barely opaque in the center when pierced with the tip of a small knife, about 6 minutes. Remove from the oven, arrange on plates, sprinkle evenly with the chives, and serve immediately.

CHEF'S NOTE: *An electric coffee grinder does a great job as a spice grinder, especially when you have to prepare a large amount of any spice, like the coarsely ground peppercorns in this recipe. Buy an inexpensive model with a revolving blade, not the type with a burr, and reserve it for grinding spices only. If you must use your coffee grinder for spices, too, grind about ¼ cup granulated sugar or raw rice to pick up residual coffee flavor, then discard the sugar or rice.*

SALT AND PEPPER CALAMARI WITH LIME CILANTRO DIP

Fried salt and pepper calamari is a staple at Southeast Asian restaurants, but this version has a Latino spin. The crusty calamari is served with a pastel green cilantro dip accented with lime. Like all fried foods, the calamari tastes best when served right after cooking, so have everyone at the table. [CHEF MICHAEL LYLE]

Serves 6

LIME CILANTRO DIP

1 cup firmly packed fresh cilantro leaves

2 tablespoons fresh lime juice

3 tablespoons extra-virgin olive oil

¾ cup mayonnaise

1 tablespoon mashed Simple Roasted Garlic (page 61)

2 teaspoons honey

1 teaspoon Sriracha chile sauce

Kosher salt

Freshly ground black pepper

¾ pound cleaned calamari bodies, cut into ½-inch-wide rings

¼ pound calamari tentacles, each section cut at the base into 3 or 4 portions

2 cups whole milk

1½ cups all-purpose flour

1 tablespoon fine sea salt

2 teaspoons freshly ground black pepper

About 6 cups vegetable oil for deep-frying

To make the Lime Cilantro Dip, put the cilantro in a food processor fitted with the metal chopping blade. With the machine running, add the lime juice, and then the oil, 1 tablespoon at a time. Add the mayonnaise, roasted garlic, honey, and chile sauce and process until thoroughly combined, stopping to scrape down the sides of the bowl with a rubber spatula as needed. Season to taste with salt and pepper. Transfer to a serving bowl, cover, and refrigerate for at least 2 hours or up to 8 hours to blend the flavors. Remove from the refrigerator about 1 hour before serving.

To ready the calamari for frying, in a large bowl, combine the calamari rings and tentacles, add the milk, and mix well. Cover with plastic wrap and refrigerate for at least 20 minutes or up to 2 hours. In another large bowl, whisk together the flour, salt, and pepper to distribute the seasonings thoroughly.

Preheat the oven to 200°F. Line a baking sheet with paper towels.

Pour the oil to a depth of at least 3 inches into a large, deep saucepan over medium-high heat and heat to 375°F on a deep-frying thermometer. Drain the calamari in a colander. Working in batches to avoid crowding the pan, coat the calamari in the flour mixture, shaking to remove the excess, and add to the hot oil. Deep-fry until the calamari is golden brown, about 3 minutes. Using a wire skimmer, transfer the calamari to the paper-lined baking sheet and keep warm in the oven while you fry the remaining calamari, always allowing the oil temperature to return to 375°F before adding more.

Transfer the calamari to a serving platter and serve hot, accompanied with the dip.

CHEF'S NOTE: *Kosher salt is the salt of choice for countless professional chefs. One of its attributes is its flaky texture, which stays on the surface of food longer before melting than fine salt, so the chef can see how much seasoning has occurred. (This quality also helps in koshering meat, as the larger crystals help leach liquid from the meat more readily.) A second plus is that it is easy to pick up a pinch between your fingers to sprinkle it on food. Most kosher salt is also pure and devoid of the additives that keep many supermarket salts "free flowing," giving it an especially clean taste.*

SILKY SALMON CONFIT

Salmon cooked in warm (not hot) oil is an unusual technique that has won many converts since it was popularized in France by chef Gérard Pangaud. The fish turns out unctuous and silky, with only salt and pepper to enhance the flavor. Stripped down as it is, be sure to use the freshest salmon, and weigh the portions accurately so they cook properly. Serve with a simple side dish, such as cherry tomatoes and asparagus in a lemon vinaigrette. [DAVID KIM]

Serves 6

1-pound center-cut salmon fillet, skin and pinbones removed

About 4 cups extra-virgin olive oil

Zest of 1 lemon, removed with a vegetable peeler

***Fleur de sel* (see Chef's Note, page 44)**

Freshly ground black pepper

Prepare the salmon fillet by carefully trimming away the blood line (the dark flesh line running along the bottom) and any dark flesh from the skinned side of the fillet. Cut the salmon in half vertically to make 2 equal portions about ½ pound each.

Place the salmon in a deep skillet just large enough to hold it without crowding. Add enough oil to cover the salmon by ¼ inch. Add the lemon zest. Place an instant-read thermometer in the oil.

Heat the oil over very low heat until it reaches 150°F and the fat lines in the salmon release small, white globules of fat on the surface of the fillet, about 20 minutes. Remove from the heat and let stand for 5 minutes. Using a large slotted spatula, carefully transfer the salmon pieces to a carving board.

Using a paring knife, gently pry apart large, individual flakes of the salmon along each of their natural separations to make large serving flakes. Using the back of the knife, carefully scrape off all of the visible fat from both sides of each flake.

Divide the salmon among 4 dinner plates, season with salt and pepper, and serve immediately.

CHEF'S NOTE: *The quality of the salmon is of the utmost importance in preparing this recipe. When shopping, insist upon wild salmon—never farm-raised. Assure that your portion is cut from the thicker area of the largest fish, as the natural marbling is important to achieving the very best results.*

SALT-CRUSTED WHOLE ROAST SEA BASS

Don't worry about the large amount of salt used here. You will be pleasantly surprised by the subtlety of the salt flavor
with your first taste of the fish. During roasting, the salt becomes a hardened shell that locks in the natural moisture of the fish and helps
to meld the herb and citrus flavors with the flesh. I use a whole striped sea bass because of its firm, thick meat and mild flavor,
but nearly any whole fish will do. [CHEF JONATHAN ROHLAND]

Serves 2

SALT CRUST

3 pounds coarse sea salt

¼ cup chopped fresh thyme

3 bay leaves, crushed

Grated zest and juice of 4 lemons

4 large egg whites

½ cup water

**1 whole striped sea bass
(about 2 pounds), cleaned**

Freshly ground black pepper

Preheat the oven to 425°F. Line a rimmed baking sheet with parchment paper.

To make the Salt Crust, in a large bowl combine the salt, thyme, bay leaves, lemon zest and juice, egg whites, and water. Using a sturdy wooden spoon, stir until well combined.

Rinse the fish, inside and out, under cold running water. Pat dry with paper towels and place on the prepared baking sheet. Season the fish on both sides with pepper. Using your hands, mound the salt mixture over the fish. Press it firmly onto the fish, enclosing the fish completely in an even layer.

Bake the fish for 25 minutes. Remove from the oven and let rest for 15 minutes.

Using a heavy spoon, crack the crust and lift off the salt in large pieces. Cut off the head and tail of the fish. Then, using a thin-bladed knife, split the exposed side of the fish lengthwise down the natural seam visible on the skin. Gently remove both halves of the top fillet to a warmed dinner plate. Lift off and discard the backbone, and remove the bottom fillet to a second warmed plate. Serve immediately.

SALT AND PEPPER–ROASTED WILD MUSHROOMS

Most supermarkets carry an interesting assortment of mushrooms, and it is worth combining a variety to experience their different flavors and textures. Roasting them with a simple seasoning of salt and pepper allows their earthy taste to shine through. This is an impressive and easy side dish for accompanying roasts, steaks, or chops. [VINCENT ROSSETTI]

Serves 4

1 teaspoon kosher salt

½ teaspoon coarsely cracked black peppercorns

6 ounces oyster mushrooms, stems trimmed

6 ounces shiitake mushrooms, stems removed and large caps halved

8 ounces cremini mushrooms, stem ends trimmed and mushrooms halved lengthwise

8 ounces white button mushrooms, stem ends trimmed and mushrooms halved lengthwise

3 cloves garlic, minced

¼ cup extra-virgin olive oil, plus more for serving

1 teaspoon chopped fresh flat-leaf parsley

Preheat the oven to 400°F.

In a small bowl, mix together the salt and pepper. In a large roasting pan, combine all of the mushrooms and the garlic. Drizzle evenly with the oil and sprinkle evenly with half of the salt and pepper mixture. Spread the mushrooms in a single layer as evenly as possible to promote even cooking.

Roast, stirring occasionally, until the edges of the mushrooms are golden brown, about 15 minutes. Remove from the oven and transfer to a serving bowl.

Season the mushrooms with the remaining salt and pepper mixture, drizzle with a little olive oil, and sprinkle with the parsley. Serve immediately.

CAJUN-SEASONED SMOKED TURKEY

This Cajun-style smoked turkey possesses sweet, spicy, and savory flavors and is a favorite with my Thanksgiving guests. Using a flavor injector (available at kitchenware stores) to pump the marinade into the turkey will distribute deep flavors throughout the flesh. [CHEF JAIME MONTILLA]

Serves 10 to 12

HONEY-SPICE MARINADE

1 cup lager beer

½ cup honey

⅓ cup cider vinegar

¼ cup Tabasco sauce

3 tablespoons Worcestershire sauce

2 teaspoons ground allspice

1 tablespoon granulated garlic

1 tablespoon granulated onion

1 tablespoon sweet paprika,
   preferably Hungarian

1 tablespoon cayenne pepper

2 tablespoons kosher salt

1 turkey (about 10 to 12 pounds),
   rinsed, trimmed of excess fat,
   and patted dry

½ cup All-Purpose Seasoning
   (page 41)

To make the Honey-Spice Marinade, in a bowl, whisk together the beer, honey, vinegar, Tabasco sauce, Worcestershire sauce, allspice, granulated garlic, granulated onion, paprika, cayenne pepper, and salt.

In batches, fill a kitchen injector with the marinade and inject it into the flesh all over the turkey. Place the turkey in a roasting pan and cover with plastic wrap. Refrigerate for at least 2 hours or up to 12 hours.

Remove the turkey from the refrigerator and pat the turkey dry with paper towels (the marinade tends to seep out). Massage the turkey all over, inside and out, with the All-Purpose Seasoning. Let the turkey stand at room temperature while you prepare the oven.

Preheat the oven to 350°F. Oil a roasting rack and place it in a roasting pan. Place the turkey, breast side up, on the prepared rack in the roasting pan.

Roast the turkey for 3¼ hours or until an instant read thermometer inserted in the thickest part of the thigh without touching the bone reads 170°F.

Remove the turkey from the oven, transfer to a large platter and let rest, tented with aluminum foil, for 30 minutes. Carve the turkey and serve hot.

GARLIC

SIMPLE ROASTED GARLIC

Having roasted garlic on hand is like having a dependable friend by your side in the kitchen.
When a savory dish lacks a little something, sweet, nutty, earthy roasted garlic can often fill the "bottom end" in the same
way that bass tones fill out the foundation of music. The technique here yields a good amount of roasted garlic with a minimum
of waste. Unlike recipes that ask the cook to squeeze the roasted pulp from its papery sheath (which can be messy),
here the garlic is peeled and trimmed before roasting. [CHEF MICHAEL NORTHERN]

Makes about 1 cup

4 large heads garlic
(see Chef's Note)

1 tablespoon extra-virgin olive oil

1 teaspoon fine sea salt

½ teaspoon freshly ground black
pepper

Preheat the oven to 375°F. Break apart the garlic heads, peel off the skins, and then carefully trim the light brown root end from each clove.

Place the garlic cloves in a single layer in a small baking dish. Drizzle evenly with the oil, and season with the salt and pepper. Pour ½ cup water over the garlic. Cover the dish securely with aluminum foil.

Bake the garlic until lightly colored and the tip of small, sharp knife pierces a clove easily, about 1 hour. Carefully remove the foil (the steam can burn you), and return the dish to the oven. Continue to bake until the garlic is a nice golden brown and the tops of the cloves look dry, 15 to 20 minutes longer. Let cool slightly, then drain off any liquid. Let cool completely.

Transfer to an airtight container and store in the refrigerator for up to 4 days. To measure the roasted garlic, mash it lightly to fit into a measuring spoon, or as directed in individual recipes.

CHEF'S NOTE: *To save time, roast store-bought peeled garlic, available in jars in the refrigerated produce section of Asian groceries and many supermarkets.*

MUSHROOM AND ROASTED GARLIC STRUDELS

Flaky, crisp, and irresistible, these individual savory strudels make a dramatic presentation.
Serve them with a green salad as a first course, a brunch dish, or a vegetarian main course, or by themselves
with cocktail plates and forks as hors d'oeuvres. Don't be intimidated by the filo dough, which has a reputation for being
difficult. The key is to let the dough thaw slowly in the refrigerator overnight. Once the package is opened, keep the filo
covered with a lightly dampened kitchen towel to prevent it from drying out. [CHEF MICHAEL PALESH]

Makes 10 small strudels

MUSHROOM FILLING

1 pound portobello mushrooms, stems removed, dark gills scraped out with the tip of a spoon, and caps cut into ¼-inch dice

½ pound shiitake mushrooms, stems removed and caps cut into ¼-inch dice

½ pound cremini mushrooms, stem ends trimmed and caps and stems cut into ¼-inch dice

4 tablespoons extra-virgin olive oil

½ cup minced shallots

¼ cup chopped fresh basil

1 teaspoon dried oregano

6 tablespoons mashed Simple Roasted Garlic (page 61)

2 tablespoons dry white wine

2 tablespoons unsalted butter

2 teaspoons kosher salt

½ teaspoon freshly ground black pepper

To make the Mushroom Filling, in a large bowl, mix together the portobello, shiitake, and cremini mushrooms. In a large skillet over medium-high heat, heat 2 tablespoons of the oil. Add ¼ cup of the shallots and cook, stirring constantly, until they begin to soften, about 15 seconds. Add half of the mushrooms and cook, stirring often, until the mushrooms give off their liquid, it evaporates, and the mushrooms are tender, about 10 minutes. Add 2 tablespoons of the basil, ½ teaspoon of the oregano, 3 tablespoons of the garlic, 1 tablespoon of the wine, and 1 tablespoon of the butter and mix well. Season to taste with 1 teaspoon of the salt and ¼ teaspoon of the pepper and remove from the heat. Spread the mixture on a large rimmed baking sheet. Repeat with the remaining half of all of the ingredients. Add to the mushrooms on the sheet and let cool completely.

Preheat the oven to 375° F. Spray a rimmed baking sheet with the cooking spray.

For each strudel, place 1 filo rectangle on a work surface, with a shorter end facing you. Brush lightly with some of the melted butter. Top with 3 more filo rectangles, brushing each one with butter. Spread ⅓ cup of the cooled mushrooms about 1 inch in from the edge of the filo stack closest to you, and form the mushrooms into a log shape. Fold the edge of the filo closest to you up to cover the mushrooms partially, fold in both sides of the filo about ½ inch, and then roll up the filo into a cylinder to enclose the filling. Place on the prepared baking sheet and brush with some of the melted butter.

Repeat with the remaining filo, mushrooms, and butter. You should have a total of 10 strudels. (The strudels can be covered loosely with plastic wrap and refrigerated for up to 2 hours before baking.)

continued >

Vegetable-oil cooking spray for
preparing the pan

20 filo sheets, each 9 by 14 inches,
thawed overnight in the
refrigerator and cut in half to
yield forty 9-by-7-inch rectangles
(see Chef's Note)

6 tablespoons unsalted butter,
melted

Finely chopped fresh chives for
garnish

Bake the strudels, occasionally rotating the baking sheet 180 degrees to ensure even browning, until they are golden brown, about 18 minutes. Serve hot, sprinkled with the chives.

CHEF'S NOTE: *Filo used to be available primarily in 1-pound boxes of 28 sheets, each measuring 17 by 14 inches, and some manufacturers still sell that size. However, many markets now also carry boxes of filo that hold two ½-pound packages, and the sheets have been shortened to 9 by 14 inches. If you have purchased a box of larger sheets, cut the sheets in half to make 40 rectangles, each measuring 8½ by 7 inches. If you are using the smaller sheets, cut into 9-by-7-inch rectangles as directed in the recipe. The slight difference in size won't make any difference when shaping the strudels.*

GARLIC LAMB CHOPS WITH VODKA, SAMBUCA, AND TARRAGON

Every New Year's Eve, I think of these lamb chops. I first served them on a special New Year's menu at a landmark Chicago restaurant, where they sold out in record time. Alcohol acts as a catalyst to release flavors in food (now you know why there is so much wine in French and Italian cooking!), so expect a real explosion of tastes here. [CHEF MICHAEL NORTHERN]

Serves 4

8 lamb loin chops, cut 1 inch thick, trimmed of excess fat

Fine sea salt

Freshly ground black pepper

3 cloves garlic, minced

2 tablespoons chopped fresh tarragon

2 tablespoons extra-virgin olive oil

¼ cup minced shallots

¼ cup vodka

¼ cup Sambuca (see Chef's Note)

¾ cup beef broth, preferably homemade, or low-sodium canned broth

2 tablespoons unsalted butter

Preheat the oven to 400°F. Season the lamb chops on both sides with 1½ teaspoons salt and ½ teaspoon pepper. Rub on both sides with the garlic, and then sprinkle with 2 teaspoons of the tarragon.

In a large, heavy-bottomed skillet over medium-high heat, heat the oil until very hot but not smoking. Add half of the lamb chops and cook until browned on the undersides, about 4 minutes. Turn the chops over and cook until browned on the second sides, about 4 minutes more. Transfer the chops to a rimmed baking sheet. Repeat with the remaining chops.

Roast the chops until an instant-read thermometer inserted horizontally into the center of a chop without touching bone reads 125°F for medium-rare, about 6 minutes. If the chops are done before the sauce is finished, transfer them to a platter and tent them with aluminum foil to keep warm.

Meanwhile, drain off all but a very thin film of fat from the skillet and return to medium-low heat. Add the shallots and stir until lightly browned, about 2 minutes. Add the vodka to the pan. Using a long-handled match, carefully light the vodka and allow it to flame until almost evaporated, about 1 minute. Add the Sambuca, light it with another match, and cook until almost evaporated, about 1 minute more.

Add the broth, increase the heat to high, and bring to a boil, scraping up the browned bits on the pan bottom with a wooden spatula. Boil until the liquid has reduced to about ¼ cup. Add the remaining 4 teaspoons tarragon and remove from the heat. Stir in the butter, 1 tablespoon at a time, to thicken the sauce slightly. Season to taste with salt and pepper.

Divide the chops among warmed dinner plates. Spoon the sauce over the chops and serve at once.

CHEF'S NOTE: *Sambuca, an Italian liqueur made from the fruit of the elder tree (genus* Sambucus, *hence the name), has a bracing aniselike flavor.*

FINGERLING POTATO SALAD
WITH POBLANO LIME VINAIGRETTE

Most potato salads are made from boiled potatoes, and there's nothing wrong with them. For a garlicky and mildly
spicy potato salad that doubles as a conversation piece, serve this recipe that uses roasted and grilled fingerling potatoes.
You will find the narrow, finger-shaped potatoes at farmers' markets and well-stocked supermarkets, often in a variety of colors,
from pale gold to russet to blue. If you like, substitute small red or white skinned potatoes. [VINCENT ROSSETTI]

Serves 4 to 6

1 pound fingerling potatoes, preferably multicolored, halved lengthwise

½ cup extra-virgin olive oil

3 cloves garlic, minced

1 teaspoon kosher salt

½ teaspoon freshly ground black pepper

½ red onion, quartered lengthwise and thinly sliced

½ pint cherry or grape tomatoes, cored and halved crosswise

⅓ cup chopped fresh cilantro

Preheat the oven to 425°F.

In a large bowl, toss the potatoes with ¼ cup of the oil and the garlic. Season with the salt and pepper. Spread the potatoes, cut side up, in a single layer on a rimmed baking sheet.

Roast the potatoes, stirring occasionally, until tender when pierced with the tip of a knife, about 18 minutes. Remove from the oven and let cool to room temperature.

Meanwhile, make the Poblano Lime Vinaigrette. In a blender, combine the chiles, lime juice, vinegar, and garlic and process until the chiles are finely chopped. With the machine running, add the oil in a thin, steady stream to form an emulsion. Season to taste with salt. Set aside.

Prepare a medium-hot fire in a charcoal grill, or preheat a gas grill on medium (see Chef's Note, page 126).

POBLANO LIME VINAIGRETTE

2 poblano chiles, roasted and peeled (see Chef's Note)

2 tablespoons fresh lime juice

1 tablespoon Champagne or white wine vinegar

1 clove garlic

½ cup extra-virgin olive oil

Kosher salt

In a large bowl, toss the potatoes with the remaining ¼ cup oil.

Place the potatoes, cut side down, on the grill and grill until they are evenly marked, 3 to 5 minutes.

Return the potatoes to the bowl and add the onion and tomatoes. Add the vinaigrette and toss to coat all of the vegetables evenly. Taste and adjust the seasoning with salt and pepper.

Scatter the cilantro over the salad and serve immediately, or cover and store at room temperature for up to 4 hours.

CHEF'S NOTE: *Some chiles and sweet peppers have tough skins that should be removed before the peppers are used. Broiling blisters the skin to make it easier to peel away. To broil, position a broiler pan about 6 inches from the source of heat. Slice off the top and bottom from the pepper, remove the stem, and set the two "lids" aside. Slit the pepper lengthwise, open it up, and discard the seeds and ribs. Place the pepper, skin side up, along with the top and bottom pieces, on the broiler pan. Broil until the skin is blackened and blistered, about 5 minutes; the timing will depend on the intensity of the heat. Don't allow any holes to burn through the peppers. Transfer to a bowl, cover securely with plastic wrap, and let steam until cool. Peel off the blackened skin.*

RACK OF LAMB WITH GARLIC HERB CRUST

This garlic-crusted lamb is beyond tender, has a refined flavor, and is simply delicious. It is perfect for entertaining guests, as long as you are sure they are garlic lovers. Ask the butcher to remove chine bone and trim away the meat and fat from the bones on each rack, a technique known as frenching. It makes the racks more attractive and easier to carve. [CHEF ALYSSA KASPAREK]

Serves 4

2 racks of lamb (about 1½ pounds each), chine bone removed and bones frenched

1½ teaspoons kosher salt

½ teaspoon freshly ground black pepper

16 large cloves garlic

¼ cup chopped fresh rosemary

2 tablespoons chopped fresh flat-leaf parsley

2 tablespoons extra-virgin olive oil

Position a rack in the lower third of the oven and preheat to 425°F.

Using a thin-bladed, sharp knife, trim the excess fat from each lamb rack, leaving a thin layer of fat. Season the lamb on all sides with the salt and pepper.

Using a chef's knife, mince the garlic, then use the side of the blade to mash it to a paste. Scrape up the garlic and transfer to a small bowl. Add the rosemary and parsley, and stir in the oil. Spread the herb mixture evenly over the trimmed top of the lamb racks. Cover the exposed rib bones with aluminum foil to keep them from burning. Place the racks, herb crust facing up, in a roasting pan. (The lamb can be prepared up to 12 hours ahead, loosely wrapped in plastic wrap, and refrigerated. Remove from the refrigerator 1 hour before roasting.)

Roast the lamb until an instant-read thermometer inserted in the thickest part of a rack without touching bone reads 125°F for medium-rare, about 25 minutes. Remove from the oven and let rest for 5 minutes.

To carve, cut between the bones to separate the rib chops. Serve immediately.

———————————————

CHEF'S NOTE: *The quality of garlic can vary dramatically throughout the year. In springtime, garlic can develop green shoots that give the cloves a pungent, harsh, overly assertive flavor. Look for firm, well-developed heads with evenly colored jackets. Avoid any that show signs of green shoots peeking out the top.*

KALUA PORK

I created this recipe to celebrate the opening of Nordstrom's first full-line retail store in Honolulu. It is a modern interpretation of a classic Hawaiian dish that traditionally calls for digging a deep pit, lining it with ti leaves, and then roasting a whole pig in it for an entire day. You won't need to dig up your yard to enjoy the great taste and flavor of this version. Serve the pork with steamed white rice to absorb the delicious juices along with a favorite green vegetable. [CHEF NAWAI KEKOOLANI]

Serves 12 to 14

1 boneless pork butt
(about 8 pounds)

¼ cup coarse Hawaiian sea salt

3 tablespoons garlic powder

2 tablespoons freshly ground
black pepper

3 cloves garlic, minced

½ cup liquid smoke

½ cup soy sauce

3 quarts water

4 or 5 ti leaves

Steamed white rice for serving

Preheat the oven to 375°F.

Pat the pork butt dry with paper towels and cut it into 6 equal pieces. Place the pieces in a Dutch oven.

In a small bowl, stir together the salt, garlic powder, pepper, minced garlic, liquid smoke, and soy sauce. Drizzle the mixture over the pork, and massage it into the meat, coating evenly. Add the water and then lay the ti leaves over the pork and liquid, overlapping them to form an even blanket. Cover the Dutch oven with aluminum foil, crimping the edges securely to form a tight seal.

Place the pan in the oven and roast until the pork is very tender when pierced with a meat fork, about 4 hours. Remove from the oven, uncover, discard the ti leaves, and let the pork rest for 20 minutes.

Using a slotted spoon, remove the pork from the pan. Pour the cooking liquid into a bowl or small pitcher and reserve the pan. Using 2 forks, pull the pork apart into finger-sized pieces. Return the meat to the pan. Pour the reserved cooking liquid over the pork and toss to moisten evenly.

Transfer the pork to a warmed large, deep bowl. Serve immediately with the rice.

CHEF'S NOTE: *Hawaiian sea salt, which is a distinctive pink, is not critical to this dish, but it does taste different—generally milder—than most sea salts. Seek out the genuine product for the most faithful rendition of this Islands' classic.*

ROASTED GARLIC BRUSCHETTA WITH TOMATO AND BASIL

Bruschetta, which is often nothing more than toasted bread rubbed with garlic and topped with tomatoes, is as simple as it is delicious. This version embellishes the original, and the pumped-up flavors will have guests clamoring for more. [CHEF TONY COLABELLI]

Serves 6 to 8

ROASTED GARLIC BRUSCHETTA

½ cup (1 stick) unsalted butter, at room temperature

⅓ cup drained, finely chopped olive oil–packed sun-dried tomatoes

⅓ cup coarsely chopped Simple Roasted Garlic (page 61)

1½ tablespoons chopped fresh basil

½ teaspoon kosher salt

Pinch of freshly ground black pepper

1 rustic-style baguette

¾ cup freshly grated Parmesan cheese, preferably Parmigiano-Reggiano

TOMATO AND BASIL TOPPING

2 large, ripe tomatoes, cored, seeded, and cut into ½-inch dice

¼ cup chopped fresh basil

3 tablespoons extra-virgin olive oil

1½ tablespoons balsamic vinegar

Kosher salt

Freshly ground black pepper

To make the Roasted Garlic Bruschetta, in a bowl, using a rubber spatula, mash together the butter, sun-dried tomatoes, roasted garlic, basil, salt, and pepper until well combined.

Split the baguette lengthwise. Spread the butter mixture over the cut surfaces, extending it to the edge of the crust. Sprinkle the buttered surfaces evenly with the Parmesan. (The prepared bread can be loosely covered with plastic wrap and stored at room temperature for up to 4 hours before continuing.)

To make the Tomato and Basil Topping, in a bowl, combine the tomatoes, basil, olive oil, and vinegar, and season with salt and pepper. Cover and let stand at room temperature for about 1 hour to blend the flavors.

Preheat the oven to 375°F.

Place the bread halves, Parmesan side up, on a large rimmed baking sheet. Bake until the cheese is nicely browned, about 10 minutes. Remove from the oven and transfer the bread halves to a cutting board.

Using a serrated knife, cut the bread into triangles and transfer them to a serving platter. Serve immediately, with the bowl of tomato topping and a slotted serving spoon on the side. Invite each guest to top the bread with a spoonful of the tomatoes.

ASPARAGUS AND ROASTED GARLIC TART

This savory tart releases a jaw-dropping aroma while it bakes. There is no better way to get appetites started than to fill the kitchen with the smell of roasted garlic. I find that using puff pastry for the crust is not only easy, but also adds a flaky texture and a buttery flavor. [CHEF MICHAEL LYLE]

Serves 8

Vegetable-oil cooking spray for preparing the pan

7 large eggs

½ cup heavy (whipping) cream

3 tablespoons mashed Simple Roasted Garlic (page 61)

2 tablespoons freshly grated Parmesan cheese, preferably Parmigiano-Reggiano

1 tablespoon finely chopped fresh chives

1 tablespoon kosher salt

¼ teaspoon freshly ground black pepper

One 12-inch square sheet frozen puff pastry, preferably all butter, thawed overnight in the refrigerator

¾ pound pencil-thin asparagus, woody stem ends removed

Preheat the oven to 350°F. Lightly spray a 10-inch tart pan with the cooking spray.

In a bowl, whisk together the eggs, cream, roasted garlic, Parmesan, chives, salt, and pepper.

Lay the puff pastry sheet on a work surface. Invert the pie pan on the pastry. Using the pan as a template, cut out a round of pastry 1½ inches wider than the circumference of the pan. Fit the pastry round into the pan. Use the back of a fork to press and decorate the edge of the crust.

Cut 6 asparagus spears into 4-inch lengths. Cut the remaining spears into 1½-inch lengths. Scatter the smaller lengths over the bottom of the pastry-lined pan, and then pour in the filling. Arrange the longer spears on the filling in a pinwheel pattern, with the tips facing outward and overlapping the stalks as needed. Place the pan on a rimmed baking sheet.

Bake the tart until the filling is puffed and lightly browned and seems set when the pan is shaken, about 40 minutes. Remove from the oven and let cool on a wire rack for 5 minutes. Cut into wedges and serve hot.

ROASTED GARLIC CHICKEN WITH CORN AND ARUGULA SALAD

Summer is the time to roast this crisp chicken because the dish also features a salad with corn, tomatoes, and arugula. But it is the earthy, mellow roasted garlic that will have your guests raving about the dish. It's easy enough to bone the chicken thighs with a boning knife, cutting the thigh bone free from the underside. Or, you can ask your butcher to bone them for you, but make sure the skin is left in place. [CHEF MICHAEL NORTHERN]

Serves 6

CHAMPAGNE VINAIGRETTE

¼ cup Champagne or white wine vinegar

1 tablespoon sugar

2 teaspoons Dijon mustard

1 shallot, quartered

1 small clove garlic, sliced

¾ cup canola oil

Kosher salt

Freshly ground white pepper

3 ears corn, shucked and silk removed

ROASTED GARLIC CHICKEN

6 skin-on, boneless chicken thighs

¼ cup mashed Simple Roasted Garlic (page 61)

1 teaspoon Worcestershire sauce

½ teaspoon Tabasco sauce

½ teaspoon kosher salt

Pinch of freshly ground black pepper

1 tablespoon extra-virgin olive oil

6 plum tomatoes, cored and cut into large chunks

10 ounces arugula leaves, tough stems removed

Kosher salt

Freshly ground black pepper

To make the Champagne Vinaigrette, in a blender, combine the vinegar, sugar, mustard, shallot, and garlic and pulse until the shallot is minced. With the machine running, add the canola oil in a thin, steady stream to form an emulsion. Season to taste with salt and pepper. Set aside.

Prepare a hot fire in a charcoal grill, or preheat a gas grill on high (see Chef's Note, page 127).

Place the corn on the grill and grill, turning as needed, until nicely browned on all sides, about 10 minutes. Remove from the grill and let cool until easy to handle.

Working with 1 ear at a time, stand it upright, stem end down, on a cutting board. Using a sharp knife, cut downward between the kernels and the cob, removing the kernels and rotating the cob a quarter turn after each cut. Discard the cobs, scoop the kernels into a bowl, and set aside.

To make the Roasted Garlic Chicken, place a chicken thigh between 2 sheets of plastic wrap. Using a flat meat mallet, pound gently, beginning from the center and working out toward the edge, until the thigh is about ½ inch thick. Transfer to a bowl. Repeat with the remaining thighs.

Add the roasted garlic, Worcestershire sauce, Tabasco sauce, salt, and pepper to the chicken and mix gently. Cover with plastic wrap and refrigerate for at least 2 hours or up to 8 hours.

In a large nonstick skillet over medium-high heat, heat the olive oil. Carefully add the chicken thighs, skin side down, and cook until the skin is deep golden brown, about 5 minutes. Turn the thighs over and cook until the undersides are lightly browned and the juices run clear when the meat is pierced with a knife, about 3 minutes longer. Transfer to a platter.

To serve, in a large bowl, combine the corn, tomatoes, and arugula. Add the vinaigrette, toss gently to coat evenly, and season to taste with salt and pepper. Transfer the salad to chilled plates, shaping the ingredients into a mound.

Using a sharp knife, slice each chicken thigh into 6 or 7 pieces. Fan out a sliced thigh on each salad. Serve immediately.

CRISP BONELESS CHICKEN WITH GARLIC HERB BUTTER

If you have been disappointed with previous attempts to roast chicken with a crackling crisp skin, this recipe will be a real find. It calls for a boned chicken (we've included instructions for boning, just in case your butcher isn't cooperative) and a two-step, skillet-to-oven cooking process. For exemplary results, use an organic bird. Mass-market chickens just aren't as tasty and the skin doesn't brown as well. You'll need a large, good-quality ovenproof skillet (such as one made by All-Clad), and an oven big enough to hold it. Your reward will be a gorgeously burnished chicken with a juicy interior—the hallmarks of a perfectly cooked bird. For a final fillip, add a dollop of intensely fragrant herb butter. [CHEF MICHAEL NORTHERN]

Serves 2 to 4

1 whole organic chicken (about 3½ pounds), boned, with wings cut off at the shoulder joint (see Chef's Note)

2 cloves garlic, minced

1 teaspoon chopped fresh rosemary

1 teaspoon chopped fresh thyme

1 teaspoon finely chopped fresh chives

3 tablespoons extra-virgin olive oil

1 teaspoon kosher salt

½ teaspoon freshly ground black pepper

GARLIC HERB BUTTER

4 tablespoons (½ stick) unsalted butter, at room temperature

2 cloves garlic, minced

1 teaspoon chopped fresh flat-leaf parsley

½ teaspoon chopped fresh rosemary

½ teaspoon chopped fresh thyme

½ teaspoon kosher salt

To prepare the chicken, one at a time, place a boneless chicken half between 2 sheets of plastic wrap. Using a flat meat mallet, gently pound the thigh and leg meat until it is as thick as the breast area. Place the chicken halves, skin side up, in a 9-by-13-inch baking dish. Rub both sides of each half with the garlic. In a small cup or bowl, mix together the rosemary, thyme, and chives, then sprinkle the herb mixture evenly over both sides of the chicken and drizzle evenly with 2 tablespoons of the oil. Cover with plastic wrap and refrigerate for at least 2 hours or up to 12 hours. About 30 minutes before cooking, remove the chicken from the refrigerator.

To make the Garlic Herb Butter, in a small bowl, combine the butter, garlic, parsley, rosemary, thyme, and salt, and mix together until the seasonings are evenly distributed. Cover and let stand at room temperature until ready to use.

Position a rack in the upper third of the oven and preheat to 450°F. Generously season the chicken halves on both sides with the salt and pepper. Smooth the chicken skins.

Add the remaining 1 tablespoon oil to a heavy-duty 12- to 14-inch ovenproof skillet over medium-high heat. Swirl to coat the bottom of the pan and heat until very hot but not smoking. Carefully place the chicken halves, skin side down, in the skillet. Cook, adjusting the heat as needed so the chicken browns steadily without burning, until the skin is golden brown, about 5 minutes. Using tongs, flip the chicken halves and continue cooking until the flesh side is lightly browned, about 3 minutes more. Transfer the chicken halves to a platter. Drain off the excess oil and return the chicken halves, skin side down, to the skillet.

Place the skillet in the oven and roast the chicken for 4 minutes, then remove from the oven. Flip the chicken halves, so they are skin side up, and return to the oven. Continue to roast until the skin is deep golden brown and an instant-read thermometer inserted in the thickest part of a breast reads 170°F, about 5 minutes more.

continued >

Place each chicken half on a dinner plate, or cut each half into breast and leg portions and divide among 4 dinner plates. Top each serving with a dollop of herb butter and serve immediately. Cover and store any leftover herb butter in the freezer for up to 1 month, and use to flavor steamed vegetables or grilled meats.

CHEF'S NOTE: *Boning a whole chicken is not difficult if you have a cleaver, poultry shears, a large knife, and a thin-bladed flexible boning knife. Practice will make perfect, and soon you will speed through the process. If you like, reserve the giblets, fat, bones, and trimmings to make stock. First, pull off any pale ivory knobs of fat at the tail area. Using the kitchen shears, cut along both sides of the backbone to remove it. Using the large knife, cut the chicken in half vertically through the keel bone. Working with 1 chicken half at a time, slip the boning knife under the rib cage to loosen it from the flesh. Using short strokes with the tip of the knife, and working toward the keel bone, cut away the rib cage, wishbone half, and keel bone. Don't worry if the tenderloin comes loose. Just place it back on the boned breast. Locate the thigh bone at the pelvis. Using the boning knife, cut away the flesh at the pelvis to expose the hip joint. Sever the hip joint, scrape the flesh away from the thigh bone to the next joint, sever it, and remove the bone. Now scrape the flesh away from the drumstick bone until you reach the end of the drumstick, and use the cleaver to chop off the bone at that point. Chop the wing at the first joint from the shoulder to remove the second joint and wing tip. Carefully rinse the chicken half and pat it completely dry with paper towels. Repeat with the remaining chicken half.*

ROASTED GARLIC SOUP WITH PULLED CHICKEN

This delicate, yet hearty soup—a version of the classic Greek *avgolemono*—will delight any garlic lover.
The flavor is deepened with caramelized Vidalia onions. Served with warm crusty bread,
it becomes a meal in a bowl. [CHEF JONATHAN ROHLAND]

Serves 6 to 8

2 boneless, skinless chicken breast halves (½ pound each)

Kosher salt

Freshly ground black pepper

4 tablespoons (½ stick) unsalted butter

2 tablespoons extra-virgin olive oil

1 large Vidalia onion, halved and thinly sliced into half-moons

3 celery stalks, finely chopped

¾ teaspoon minced fresh thyme

2 bay leaves

½ cup dry white wine

1 can (49 ounces) low-sodium chicken broth

1 cup whole Simple Roasted Garlic cloves (page 61)

1½ cups heavy (whipping) cream

2 tablespoons all-purpose flour

3 tablespoons fresh lemon juice

2 teaspoons chopped fresh sage

Freshly grated Parmesan cheese, preferably Parmigiano-Reggiano, for garnish

Preheat the oven to 350°F.

Pat the chicken breasts dry with a paper towel. Season the breasts all over with 1½ teaspoons salt and ½ teaspoon pepper.

In a soup pot over medium-low heat, melt 2 tablespoons of the butter with the oil. Increase the heat to high. Add the chicken breasts and cook until the undersides are nicely browned, about 2 minutes. Turn the breasts and brown the second sides, about 2 minutes more. Transfer the breasts to a rimmed baking sheet. Reserve the soup pot.

Roast until an instant-read thermometer inserted in the thickest part of a breast reads 165°F, about 20 minutes. Remove from the oven and let cool until easy to handle. Using your fingers, pull the chicken into fine strands. Place in a bowl, cover, and refrigerate until ready to use.

While the chicken is roasting, add the onion to the fat remaining in the pot and cook over medium heat, stirring occasionally, until golden brown, about 15 minutes. Add the celery, thyme, and bay leaves and continue to cook until the celery is tender and fragrant, about 3 minutes. Add the wine and cook until almost evaporated, about 4 minutes. Add the broth and roasted garlic and bring just to a simmer. Reduce the heat to medium-low and simmer gently for about 20 minutes to blend the flavors. Remove the bay leaves. Stir in the cream, increase the heat to medium, and return the mixture to a simmer.

In a saucepan over medium-low heat, melt the remaining 2 tablespoons butter. Whisk in the flour and let bubble without browning for 1 minute. Whisk in 2 cups of the soup, then whisk this mixture into the soup. Add the reserved chicken and lemon juice, bring back to a simmer, and cook, stirring occasionally, until the soup is lightly thickened and the chicken is heated through. Season to taste with salt and pepper.

Ladle the soup into warmed bowls and sprinkle each serving with sage and Parmesan. Serve at once.

CHILE AND SPICE

THAI CRAB SALAD WITH SPICY DRESSING

For a fantastic main-course salad at a summer party, serve this cool and colorful Thai dish. Its secret lies in the dressing, which provides wonderful flavor with an intriguing combination of spicy, sweet, and tart. Fresh lime juice is imperative, and be sure to include the pulp to provide a bit of extra tang. You can also make this salad with cooked shrimp in addition to, or instead of, the crab, or offer it in smaller portions as a first course. [CHEF JOHN BARRON]

Serves 6 to 8

SPICY THAI DRESSING

⅓ cup fresh lime juice, including pulp

2 tablespoons Asian fish sauce

¼ cup sugar

2 tablespoons honey

2 tablespoons *sambal oelek*

2 cloves garlic, minced

1 tablespoon Asian sesame oil

½ cup peanut oil

4 cups shredded green cabbage

1¼ cups shredded red cabbage

2 cups packed mesclun (mixed baby salad greens)

2 mangoes, pitted, peeled, and cut into ½-inch dice

1 carrot, peeled and cut into very thin julienne strips

4 large plum tomatoes, cored, seeded, and cut lengthwise into ¼-inch-wide strips

3 tablespoons thinly sliced fresh mint ribbons

¼ cup thinly sliced fresh Thai or Italian basil leaves

1 pound crabmeat, preferably Dungeness, picked over for shell bits

To make the Spicy Thai Dressing, in a blender, combine the lime juice with its pulp, fish sauce, sugar, honey, *sambal oelek,* and garlic and process to dissolve the sugar. With the machine running, add the sesame oil, and then add the peanut oil in a thin, steady stream to form an emulsion. Transfer to a container, cover with plastic wrap, and set aside.

In a large bowl, combine the green and red cabbage, mesclun, mangoes, carrot, tomatoes, mint, basil, and crab and toss to mix. Add the dressing and toss to coat evenly.

Using tongs, transfer the salad to chilled bowls, shaping the ingredients into a mound. Serve immediately.

CHEF'S NOTE: *Fish sauce, made from various fermented fish and shellfish, is an essential ingredient in the cooking of Thailand and Vietnam, where it is called* nam pla *and* nuoc mam, *respectively. Sambal oelek, which looks like a bright red Asian salsa, is a condiment made from ground hot chiles. One popular brand of Sambal has a drawing of a rooster on the label. You can find both products at Asian markets and many supermarkets.*

CILANTRO LIME CHICKEN TACOS

These are not your typical chicken tacos. In many of our restaurants, we have a popular chicken salad that is dressed with a unique cilantro and lime vinaigrette. That dressing is put to good use here as a condiment for brightly colored—and flavored—tacos. Purchase ground chicken that includes all dark meat, rather than breast meat only, or the taco filling will be too dry. When preparing this recipe, use both the stems and the leaves of the cilantro. And be sure to use the dressing within a few hours of preparation, as the flavor and the color diminish noticeably when held overnight. [CHEF MICHAEL NORTHERN]

Serves 4 to 6

CILANTRO LIME VINAIGRETTE

3 tablespoons seasoned rice vinegar

2 tablespoons fresh lime juice

1 tablespoon honey

1 small clove garlic, minced

1 teaspoon minced chipotle chile in adobo sauce

Pinch of kosher salt

⅓ cup plus 1 tablespoon canola oil

½ cup chopped fresh cilantro

CHICKEN TACO FILLING

2 tablespoons canola oil

1 pound ground dark-meat chicken

½ cup chopped fresh cilantro

2 cloves garlic, minced

1½ teaspoons kosher salt

½ teaspoon freshly ground black pepper

2 tablespoons fresh lime juice

1 tablespoon soy sauce

12 taco shells

½ head romaine lettuce, finely shredded crosswise

4 plum tomatoes, cored, seeded, and cut into ½-inch dice (about 1 cup)

⅓ cup finely chopped yellow bell pepper

1 cup crumbled *queso fresco*

Fresh cilantro sprigs for garnish

To make the Cilantro Lime Vinaigrette, in a blender, combine the vinegar, lime juice, honey, garlic, chile, and salt and process until smooth. With the machine running, add the oil in a thin, steady stream to form an emulsion. Add the cilantro and process until the vinaigrette is deep green with small flecks of cilantro. Taste and adjust the seasoning, then set aside.

To make the Chicken Taco Filling, in a large skillet over medium-high heat, heat the oil. Add the chicken, cilantro, garlic, salt, and pepper and cook, stirring and breaking up any chunks with a wooden spatula, until the chicken shows no sign of pink, about 8 minutes. Reduce the heat to medium-low. Stir in the lime juice and soy sauce and cook until they are almost evaporated, about 1 minute. Remove from the heat.

To assemble the tacos, divide the chicken mixture evenly among the taco shells. Top with the lettuce and drizzle each taco with about 1 tablespoon of the vinaigrette. Add a scattering of tomato and yellow pepper, and garnish with some of the cheese and a cilantro sprig. Serve immediately, and pass the remaining vinaigrette at the table.

CHEF'S NOTE: *The same ingredients used for these tacos can be used to make tostadas. Simply replace the taco shells with flat fried tortillas and assemble in the same manner.*

SPICY HONEY CHIPOTLE GLAZED CHICKEN BREAST

There is more than one way to roast a chicken. Soaking the poultry in brine before roasting infuses the meat with flavorful liquid that keeps it moist even in a hot oven. In this recipe, a sweet and spicy glaze delivers a tasty finish. If you can get your butcher to prepare the chicken breasts with the wing attached, they make an eye-catching presentation. [CHEF DANIEL WOOD]

Serves 6

CILANTRO BRINE

1½ teaspoons cumin seeds

1½ teaspoons black peppercorns

2 bay leaves

½ cup kosher salt

¼ cup firmly packed light brown sugar

½ cup firmly packed fresh cilantro stems (reserve the leaves for the glaze)

2 cups ice cubes

6 skin-on, bone-in chicken breast halves (10 ounces each)

HONEY CHIPOTLE GLAZE

½ cup honey

¼ cup fresh lime juice

¼ cup coarsely chopped fresh cilantro

1 tablespoon finely chopped chipotle chile in adobo sauce, with any clinging sauce

1 small clove garlic, coarsely chopped

Kosher salt

Freshly ground black pepper

¼ cup extra-virgin olive oil

½ cup loosely packed fresh cilantro leaves

To make the Cilantro Brine, heat a medium saucepan over medium heat until hot. Add the cumin, peppercorns, and bay leaves and cook, stirring often, until toasted and fragrant, about 3 minutes. Add 6 cups water, the salt, sugar, and cilantro stems. Bring to a boil and then reduce the heat to low. Simmer, stirring often, until the sugar and salt are dissolved, about 10 minutes. Pour into a large stainless-steel or heatproof glass bowl. Add the ice cubes and stir until they have melted and the broth is cool. Add the chicken breasts, cover, and refrigerate for at least 2 hours or up to 6 hours.

Meanwhile, make the Honey Chipotle Glaze. In a blender, combine the honey, lime juice, cilantro, chile, and garlic and process until smooth. Season to taste with salt and pepper. Set aside.

Preheat the oven to 375°F. Remove the chicken from the brine and dry well with paper towels. In a large ovenproof skillet over high heat, heat the olive oil. Working in batches to prevent crowding, place the chicken, skin side down, in the skillet and cook until the skin is well browned and crisp, about 6 minutes. Turn the chicken over and cook until lightly browned on the second sides, about 2 minutes more. Transfer to a plate and repeat with the remaining chicken breasts.

When all of the chicken breasts have been browned, return them, skin side up, to the skillet. Brush with some of the glaze and reserve the remaining glaze. Place the skillet in the oven and roast until an instant-read thermometer inserted in the thickest part of a breast without touching bone reads 165°F, about 20 minutes.

Remove the chicken breasts from the oven and brush with the remaining glaze. Transfer to a platter and let rest for 5 minutes. Scatter the cilantro leaves over the chicken, and serve hot.

CHEF'S NOTE: *The smoky, intensely hot flavor of chipotle chiles has gone from a somewhat esoteric taste thrill to a national addiction. Chipotles are fully ripened red jalapeño chiles that have been dried by smoking them over a fire. They are sold whole, ground into a powder, or whole canned in a vinegary adobo sauce. Canned chipotles, which are found in Latin markets and many supermarkets, are very spicy, and you may want to wear gloves to protect your skin when handling them. To use the canned chiles, remove them and any clinging adobo from the can and place on a cutting board to chop. While it is true that the chile seeds hold much of the heat, don't bother to remove them from a canned chipotle. You don't use this chile without expecting plenty of spice. To store leftover canned chipotles, transfer them to a small airtight container and refrigerate for up to a few weeks. Or, freeze them: Spoon each chile with its sauce onto a waxed paper–lined baking sheet and freeze until solid. Slip each frozen chile and sauce into a small lock-top plastic bag and freeze for up to 3 months.*

FIVE SPICE-SEARED AHI TUNA

Seared tuna steak makes a perfect light meal. The clean yet spicy flavor of the marinade and the mild zest of the five-spice powder make this tuna easy to partner with a simple side dish, such as a mixed green salad with an Asian vinaigrette or a soba noodle salad dressed with soy sauce and ginger. Be careful not to marinate the tuna longer than directed, or the flesh will "cook" in the soy sauce. [MICHAEL THOMS]

Serves 4

¼ cup soy sauce

1 teaspoon Asian chile oil

1 teaspoon Sriracha chile sauce

¼ teaspoon garlic powder

4 sushi-grade tuna steaks, each 6 ounces and ¾ inch thick

2 teaspoons Chinese five-spice powder

2 tablespoons canola oil

Asian sesame oil for serving

In a shallow bowl, whisk together the soy sauce, chile oil, chile sauce, and garlic powder. One at a time, add the tuna steaks to the marinade, turn to coat thoroughly, and place in an 8-by-11½-inch glass baking dish. Pour the marinade over the tuna. Cover and refrigerate for 45 minutes, turning the tuna in the marinade after 15 minutes. Remove the tuna from the marinade and drain briefly on paper towels. Season the tuna on both sides with the five-spice powder.

In a large, heavy skillet over medium-high heat, heat the oil until very hot but not smoking. Add the tuna steaks and cook until the undersides are seared, about 3 minutes. Turn the steaks and cook until the second sides are seared, about 2 minutes more for rare tuna.

Transfer the tuna steaks to warmed dinner plates. Drizzle with the sesame oil and serve immediately.

CHEF'S NOTE: *Sriracha (pronounced SEE-rah-cha) sauce is an all-purpose Southeast Asian hot sauce made from sun-ripened ground chiles, vinegar, sugar, and garlic. It originated in southern Thailand, but you can now find an especially spicy American brand (in a squeeze bottle with a rooster on the label) at Asian markets and many supermarkets. The imported Thai brands are somewhat milder and have a more sweet-and-sour note.*

HONEYED PORK TENDERLOIN WITH APPLE CHILE CHUTNEY

Pork tenderloin is one of the leanest meats available. Here, it is rubbed with honey and spices and roasted,
and then served with a sweet and spicy apple chutney made from Gala apples, superb dessert apples that are also good for
making this savory condiment. I prepare the chutney and allow it to rest while I season and roast the tenderloins.
That way, the tenderloins are carved while they are still juicy and tender. [CHEF RICHARD VENZOR]

Serves 4 to 6

APPLE CHILE CHUTNEY

**4 Gala apples, cored, peeled, and
cut into ½-inch dice**

1 cup cider vinegar

1 cup firmly packed light brown sugar

1 cup minced red onion

**¼ cup seeded, deribbed, and finely
chopped poblano chiles**

3 tablespoons honey

2 teaspoons ground ginger

1 teaspoon kosher salt

PORK RUB

1½ tablespoons light brown sugar

1 tablespoon chili powder

1½ teaspoons granulated garlic

**1½ teaspoons sweet paprika,
preferably Hungarian**

1½ teaspoons dry mustard

½ teaspoon ground cumin

½ teaspoon cayenne pepper

**½ teaspoon freshly ground white
pepper**

½ teaspoon kosher salt

**Vegetable-oil cooking spray for
preparing the pan**

**2 boneless pork tenderloins (about
1 pound each), silver skin trimmed**

¼ cup honey

To make the Apple Chile Chutney, in a heavy saucepan over medium heat, combine the apples, vinegar, sugar, onion, chiles, honey, ginger, and salt. Bring to a boil, stirring often. Reduce the heat to medium-low and simmer until the apples are very tender and the juices are syrupy, about 30 minutes. Remove from the heat and let cool completely. (The chutney can be made up to 2 days ahead, cooled, covered, and refrigerated. Bring to room temperature before serving.)

To make the Pork Rub, in a small bowl, stir together the sugar, chili powder, granulated garlic, paprika, mustard, cumin, cayenne, white pepper, and salt. Set aside.

Position a rack in the lower third of the oven and preheat to 450°F. Spray a large nonstick roasting pan with cooking spray.

Brush the pork tenderloins all over with the honey, coat them with the rub, and place them in the prepared pan. Roast for 10 minutes. Reduce the oven temperature to 400°F and continue roasting until an instant-read thermometer inserted in the center of a tenderloin reads 150°F for medium-well, about 10 minutes more. Transfer the tenderloins to a carving board, tent them with foil, and let rest for 5 minutes.

Cut the tenderloins crosswise into ½-inch-thick slices. Serve immediately on warmed dinner plates, with a spoonful of chutney added to each plate.

CHEF'S NOTE: *Not all chiles are fiery hot. Deep green, triangular poblano chiles have a heat level that falls somewhere between a bell pepper and a jalapeño chile. They are sometimes labeled ancho, but that term should be reserved for the dried poblano, which is brownish red.*

JALAPEÑO CHEDDAR CORN BREAD

In the South, even the best meal is considered that much better when freshly baked corn bread is served.
My version takes a classic recipe and adds zippy jalapeños and sharp Cheddar cheese. Served sizzling from a cast-iron skillet,
there are few things that I enjoy more. [CHEF JONATHAN ROHLAND]

Serves 8

1 cup (2 sticks) unsalted butter,
   at room temperature

¾ cup sugar

4 large eggs

1 cup all-purpose flour

1 cup yellow cornmeal

4 teaspoons baking powder

1½ teaspoons kosher salt

Pinch of freshly ground black pepper

1 cup fresh or frozen corn kernels

½ cup heavy (whipping) cream

1½ cups (6 ounces) shredded sharp
   Cheddar cheese

3 jalapeño chiles, seeded, deribbed,
   and thinly sliced

¼ cup extra-virgin olive oil

Preheat the oven to 400°F. Place a 10-inch cast-iron skillet into the oven to heat until very hot.

In a large bowl, using an electric mixer set on high speed, cream together the butter and sugar until pale yellow, about 3 minutes. Beat in the eggs, one at a time, beating well after each addition until incorporated.

In another bowl, whisk together the flour, cornmeal, baking powder, salt, and pepper. Add to the butter mixture and stir with a wooden spoon just until combined (the batter will look lumpy.) Fold in the corn and then the cream just to moisten and barely smooth out the batter. Finally, fold in the cheese and jalapeños just until evenly distributed. Do not overbeat the batter.

Remove the skillet from the oven, add the oil, and swirl it to coat the bottom and sides of the skillet. Pour the batter into the hot skillet and smooth the top with the wooden spoon.

Return the skillet to the oven and bake the bread until a wooden toothpick inserted in the center comes out clean, about 45 minutes.

Cut into wedges and serve hot.

CHEF'S NOTE: *A cast-iron skillet is a great pan to own. Its heavy, thick construction holds heat beautifully. Most new cast-iron skillets are sold already seasoned (the cast iron needs to be impregnated with vegetable oil before using). Never wash cast-iron cookware in soap and water. Detergents will remove the oils that make the surface nonstick, causing the iron to rust. Instead, rinse the skillet in hot water, add a handful of salt, and use the salt and a wad of paper towels to rub out any cooked-on food. Then rinse the skillet and dry well before storing.*

KUNG PAO CALAMARI

According to Chinese legend, *kung pao* means "guardian of the throne" and is named for the general who was in charge of protecting the emperor. To most American cooks, it means "Chinese takeout!" This popular dish is easy enough to make at home. Here it is made with calamari, rather than the more familiar chicken or shrimp. [CHEF RICHARD SILVA]

Serves 6

MARINADE

1 tablespoon dry white wine

1 tablespoon soy sauce

1 tablespoon Asian sesame oil

1 pound calamari steaks, cut into ¾-inch chunks

SAUCE

1 tablespoon chile garlic sauce

1 tablespoon dry white wine

1 tablespoon soy sauce

1 tablespoon Asian sesame oil

¼ cup low-sodium chicken broth

1 teaspoon distilled white vinegar

1 tablespoon cornstarch dissolved in 1 tablespoon cold water

3 tablespoons peanut oil

4 dried chiles

2 tablespoons julienned fresh ginger

2 teaspoons minced garlic

4 green onions, cut into 1-inch lengths

½ small yellow onion, cut into 1-inch chunks

1 small red bell pepper, diced

1 small yellow bell pepper, diced

1 can (8 ounces) whole water chestnuts, rinsed, drained, and quartered

1 cup (about 4 ounces) chopped dry-roasted peanuts

Hot steamed rice for serving

To make the Marinade, in a small bowl, whisk together the wine, soy sauce, and sesame oil. Add the calamari and toss to coat. Cover and refrigerate for at least 20 minutes and no longer than 30 minutes.

Meanwhile, make the Sauce. In a small bowl, whisk together the chile sauce, wine, soy sauce, sesame oil, broth, and vinegar. Pour into a skillet, place over low heat, and bring just to a simmer, stirring often, about 5 minutes. Remove from the heat and stir in the dissolved cornstarch. Set aside.

Drain the calamari in a colander. In a very large skillet or wok over high heat, heat 1½ tablespoons of the peanut oil until it begins to smoke. Add the chiles, ginger, garlic, and green onions and cook, stirring constantly, until fragrant, about 1 minute. Add the calamari and stir-fry until seared but not quite cooked through, about 3 minutes. Transfer the calamari mixture to a bowl.

Return the skillet to high heat. Add the remaining 1½ tablespoons peanut oil and heat until very hot. Add the yellow onion, red and yellow bell peppers, water chestnuts, and peanuts and stir-fry until the vegetables are crisp-tender, about 3 minutes. Return the calamari to the skillet and stir-fry to combine the flavors, about 1 minute. Stir in the sauce and cook, stirring, until it thickens, about 30 seconds.

Spoon the rice into bowls and top with the calamari and vegetables. Serve hot.

SPICY ASIAN-MARINATED VEAL CHOP

Sweet and spicy, this marinade will add a bold layer of flavor to just about whatever you choose to soak in it.
Here, it is paired with thick veal rib chops, but pork, chicken, fish, or vegetables would also work beautifully.
Try it as a marinade for grilled foods, too. [CHEF MICHAEL LYLE]

Serves 4

MONGOLIAN MARINADE

½ cup white wine vinegar

⅓ cup (about 1½ ounces) chopped
dry-roasted peanuts

⅓ cup honey

¼ cup hoisin sauce

¼ cup low-sodium soy sauce

¼ cup Asian sesame oil

¼ cup Chinese plum sauce

¼ cup Sriracha chile sauce

4 cloves garlic, minced

2 tablespoons minced shallot

2 tablespoons peeled and minced
fresh ginger

2 tablespoons finely chopped fresh
cilantro

4 veal rib chops (about ¾ pound
each)

2 teaspoons kosher salt

¾ teaspoon freshly ground black
pepper

3 tablespoons peanut oil

To make the Mongolian Marinade, in a bowl, whisk together the vinegar, peanuts, honey, hoisin sauce, soy sauce, sesame oil, plum sauce, chile sauce, garlic, shallot, ginger, and cilantro. Place the veal chops in a 1-gallon lock-top plastic bag and pour in the marinade. Squeeze out all of the air and seal the bag. Refrigerate the bag, turning it occasionally, for at least 12 hours or up to 18 hours.

Preheat the oven to 400°F.

Remove the chops from the marinade. Measure 2 cups of the marinade and transfer to a saucepan. Bring to a boil over high heat, reduce the heat to low, and simmer until reduced to about 1⅓ cups, about 20 minutes. Keep warm to serve as a sauce.

Meanwhile, pat the chops dry with paper towels. Season the chops on both sides with the salt and pepper. In a very large ovenproof skillet, preferably nonstick, over medium-high heat, heat the peanut oil. Add the chops and cook until the undersides are nicely browned, about 3 minutes. Turn the chops and transfer the skillet to the oven. Roast until an instant-read thermometer inserted horizontally into the center of a chop without touching bone reads 135°F for medium, about 10 minutes.

Transfer the chops to warmed dinner plates and let rest for a few minutes. Spoon some of the sauce around each chop and serve immediately.

MUSSELS, CLAMS, AND SHRIMP IN SPICY TOMATO BROTH

I grew up in San Francisco, where the seafood stew known as cioppino is on many restaurant menus.
It can be a somewhat complicated dish, but with a few adjustments, it can be prepared easily at home to take advantage
of shellfish available at most supermarkets. Be sure there is plenty of crusty sourdough bread to sop up all of the
spicy red pepper–flecked broth. [CHEF ALYSSA KASPAREK]

Serves 4

¼ cup extra-virgin olive oil

½ yellow onion, thinly sliced into
half-moons

6 cloves garlic, minced

1½ teaspoons red pepper flakes

1 bay leaf

1 cup dry white wine

1 can (28 ounces) fire-roasted diced
tomatoes in juice

1 bottle (8 ounces) clam juice

24 littleneck or Manila clams
(about 2½ pounds), scrubbed

24 mussels (about 2 pounds),
scrubbed and debearded
if necessary

Grated zest of 1 lemon

24 large (21/25 count) shrimp
(about 1 pound), peeled and
deveined

½ cup thinly sliced fresh basil leaves

Kosher salt

Freshly ground black pepper

In a large saucepan over medium heat, heat the oil. Add the onion and cook, stirring, until translucent, about 5 minutes. Add the garlic, red pepper flakes, and bay leaf and cook, stirring, until the garlic is fragrant, about 2 minutes. Add the wine, bring to a boil, and cook until the wine has almost evaporated, about 5 minutes.

Add the tomatoes with their juice and the clam juice and bring to a simmer. Reduce the heat to medium-low and simmer, stirring occasionally, until the tomatoes soften, about 8 minutes. Discard any open clams or mussels that don't close when rapped. Add the lemon zest and the clams, cover, and increase the heat to high. Cook for 3 minutes. Add the mussels, re-cover, and cook until both the clams and the mussels open, about 5 minutes more. Using tongs and a slotted spoon, transfer the opened shellfish to warmed individual bowls, discarding any shellfish that did not open. Add the shrimp to the broth and cook just until they turn opaque, about 3 minutes.

Remove the bay leaf, stir in the basil, and season with salt and pepper. Spoon equal amounts of the shrimp and broth into the bowls over the opened shellfish. Serve hot.

CHEF'S NOTE: *The key to this dish is to cook the seafood in stages. Otherwise, some of the seafood will overcook and be tough.*

CRISPY SHORT RIBS WITH SZECHUAN GLAZE

This recipe answers an age-old question: What can I do with the leftovers? Here, I draw on another recipe in this book,
Slow-Braised Short Ribs (page 165). What begins as a tender and comforting stew is transformed into crisp morsels with an amped-up
Chinese barbecue sauce. Refrigerate the leftover sauce in a jar for up to a month and use it to deliver a blast of flavor to
just about anything. Grilled Whole Chicken with Szechuan Glaze (page 98) is a good example of what it can do.
Accompany the ribs with stir-fried vegetables and steamed white rice. [CHEF MICHAEL NORTHERN]

Serves 4

SZECHUAN GLAZE

2 tablespoons canola oil

3 cloves garlic, minced

1 tablespoon peeled and minced
    fresh ginger

1 tablespoon Chinese chile sauce
    with garlic

½ cup seasoned rice vinegar

2 cups hoisin sauce

¼ cup soy sauce

½ cup chopped fresh cilantro

About 6 cups canola oil for
    deep-frying

4½ cups (1½ pounds) boneless meat
    from Slow-Braised Short Ribs
    (page 165), cut into ¾-inch cubes

1 teaspoon toasted sesame seeds

1 tablespoon finely diced red bell
    pepper

Fresh cilantro sprigs for garnish

To make the Szechuan Glaze, in a saucepan over medium-low heat, heat the oil. Add the garlic, ginger, and chile sauce and cook, stirring, until the mixture is fragrant, about 1 minute. Add the vinegar and cook until almost evaporated, about 5 minutes. Reduce the heat to low, add the hoisin and soy sauces, and cook, stirring constantly, until well blended, about 5 minutes. The glaze should be a little thicker than bottled barbecue sauce. Dilute with a little water, if necessary. Remove from the heat and let cool completely. Stir in the chopped cilantro. (The glaze can be made up to 1 week ahead, cooled, and stored in a covered jar in the refrigerator.)

Pour the oil to a depth of at least 3 inches into a large, deep saucepan over medium-high heat and heat to 375°F on a deep-frying thermometer. Line a baking sheet with paper towels.

Carefully add half of the short rib cubes to the hot oil and fry, stirring occasionally, until deeply browned and crisp, about 8 minutes. Using a slotted spoon or a wire skimmer, transfer the beef cubes to the towel-lined baking sheet to drain. Set aside in a warm place. Repeat with the remaining beef cubes.

Transfer the crisp fried beef cubes to a bowl and drizzle ½ cup plus 2 tablespoons of the glaze over the cubes. Using a spoon, stir and fold to coat the cubes evenly with the glaze.

Transfer the coated cubes to a serving platter, stacking them and building height in the center. Sprinkle the sesame seeds and bell pepper over the mound, and top with a few cilantro sprigs. Serve immediately.

CHEF'S NOTE: *Hoisin sauce is a thick, sweetened, spiced soybean sauce sold in jars or cans. You can find it at most supermarkets, but because you need 2 cups for this recipe, it will be more economical to purchase it at an Asian grocery.*

GRILLED WHOLE CHICKEN WITH SZECHUAN GLAZE

Barbecued chicken can be a little too predictable. Thanks to the deep flavors in the Szechuan Glaze, this grilled chicken delivers the sweet, earthy, spicy flavors that people look for in great barbecue. Serve it with a sweet white wine, such as a Riesling or Gewürztraminer. [RICHARD LADD]

Serves 6

1 whole chicken (about 5 pounds), preferably organic

3 large cloves garlic, crushed with the flat side of a knife blade

1 lime, quartered

½ cup plus 2 tablespoons Szechuan Glaze (page 97)

1½ teaspoons kosher salt

½ teaspoon freshly ground black pepper

Vegetable oil for preparing the roasting rack

Chinese chile sauce with garlic for serving

Rinse the chicken under cold running water and pat dry. Stuff the body cavity with the garlic, lime wedges, and 2 tablespoons of the Szechuan Glaze. Using kitchen string, tie the drumsticks together and tie the wings to the body. Mix together the salt and pepper, and season the bird all over with the mixture. Let the chicken stand at room temperature while you prepare the grill.

Prepare an indirect fire in a charcoal or gas grill (see Chef's Note, page 106).

Oil a roasting rack and place it in a disposable aluminum foil pan. Put the chicken, breast side down, on the rack, and then place the pan on the cooking grate over the empty side of the charcoal grill or the turned-off burners of the gas grill. Cover and grill the chicken for 1 hour. Turn the chicken breast side up. If using a charcoal grill, add 10 fresh briquettes to the coals to maintain an even temperature. Re-cover the grill and continue grilling until an instant-read thermometer inserted in the thigh without touching bone reads 170°F, about 45 minutes more. During the last 20 minutes of grilling, brush the chicken generously with some of the remaining glaze. Pour any remaining glaze into a small saucepan and set aside.

Transfer the chicken to a carving board and let rest for 10 minutes. Then cut up the chicken to yield 2 drumsticks, 2 thighs, 2 breast halves, and 2 wings, capturing any released juices. Transfer the chicken pieces to a platter. Stir the carving juices into the reserved glaze, bring to a simmer over medium heat, and pour into a warmed bowl.

Serve the chicken immediately. Pass the glaze and the chile sauce at the table.

THAI CHICKEN AND RICE NOODLE SOUP

Have you ever wondered why spicy soups are so popular in warm climates, even when the temperature is soaring? The spices in the food increase your internal temperature, causing perspiration and making your personal natural cooling mechanism kick in. This Thai soup is milder than what you would be served at a food stall in the streets of Bangkok, but it still has an enjoyable amount of heat. Add more chiles if you are a hothead like me. [CHEF DANIEL WOOD]

Serves 4

1 tablespoon vegetable oil

2 serrano chiles, seeded, deribbed, and finely chopped

2 cloves garlic, thinly sliced lengthwise

3 kaffir lime leaves, cut lengthwise into very fine ribbons (see Chef's Note)

One 3-inch piece lemongrass stalk, tender inner bulb only, minced

5 cardamom pods

½ small yellow onion, cut into ¼-inch dice

1 small carrot, peeled and cut into ¼-inch dice

4 cups low-sodium chicken broth

Kosher salt

2 chicken breast fillets (6 ounces each)

¼ pound fresh thin rice noodles (see Chef's Note)

2 cups packed baby spinach leaves

⅓ cup fresh lime juice

3 tablespoons Asian fish sauce (see Chef's Note, page 83)

1 tablespoon Sriracha chile sauce

Kosher salt

Freshly ground black pepper

Fresh cilantro leaves for garnish

1 lime, cut into wedges

In a soup pot over medium heat, heat the oil. Add the chiles, garlic, lime leaves, lemongrass, and cardamom and cook, stirring, until the mixture is fragrant, about 1 minute. Add the onion and carrot and cook, stirring almost constantly, until tender, about 4 minutes. Add the broth and 2 teaspoons salt, cover, and bring to a boil. Reduce the heat to low, add the chicken fillets, cover, and simmer until the chicken is cooked through, about 12 minutes. Using a slotted spoon, transfer the chicken to a plate and set aside. Scoop out the cardamom pods and discard them.

Increase the heat to high and bring the broth to a boil. Stir in the noodles and cook until tender, about 2 minutes. Meanwhile, using a fork, shred the chicken. Stir the chicken, spinach, lime juice, fish sauce, and chile sauce into the soup. Cook just until the chicken is heated through, about 1 minute. Season the soup to taste with salt and pepper.

Ladle the soup into warmed large bowls. Top with the cilantro leaves and serve immediately. Pass the lime wedges at the table for squeezing into the soup.

CHEF'S NOTE: *Kaffir lime leaves, which have a lovely citrus aroma and flavor, can be found in the refrigerated or freezer section of Southeast Asian and Indian markets. If unavailable, substitute the grated zest of 1 lime.*

Fresh rice noodles are available at Asian markets. If you can't find them, look for dried rice noodles (often called rice vermicelli), which are stocked in most supermarkets. To use the dried noodles, place them in a large bowl and add hot tap water to cover by ½ inch. Let stand until the noodles are tender, 10 to 15 minutes, and then drain well. Add them to the soup and cook just until heated through, about 1 minute. Ladle the soup into warmed bowls, garnish each serving with a scattering of cilantro leaves, and serve with lime wedges for passing.

SMOKE AND COALS

FIVE SPICE–LACQUERED SPARERIBS **105**

GRILLED CHICKEN PIRI-PIRI **107**

CUBAN SMOKED PORK SHOULDER **108**

TEQUILA CHICKEN SKEWERS WITH PINEAPPLE MANGO CHUTNEY **110**

GRILLED CAPRESE PIZZA WITH ROSEMARY PARMESAN CRUST **113**

ANCHO PORK CHOPS WITH LIME DRIZZLE **115**

TOMATO AND GRILLED BREAD SALAD **116**

HERB-GRILLED VEGETABLE SALAD WITH GOAT CHEESE **119**

CILANTRO LIME GRILLED SHRIMP **121**

LONE STAR RIB-EYE STEAK **122**

GRILLED DIVER SCALLOPS WITH ROASTED-TOMATO BUTTER SAUCE **125**

GRILLED SKIRT STEAK WITH CHIMICHURRI **127**

APPLE WOOD–SMOKED LOBSTER **128**

FIVE SPICE–LACQUERED SPARERIBS

Five-spice powder, a popular southern Chinese seasoning that typically mixes Szechuan peppercorns, star anise, cinnamon, fennel seeds, and cloves, is an especially good match with pork. When grilling first-class spareribs, there are no shortcuts. Here, the ribs are smeared with a spice rub, slowly smoked with apple wood, and then finished with a sweet glaze. You'll find the five-spice powder and the *char siu* sauce (a honey-based Chinese "barbecue sauce") at Asian markets. And a grill rib rack, available at kitchenware stores, will hold this large quantity of ribs over the fire without crowding. [CHEF DANIEL WOOD]

Serves 6

FIVE-SPICE GLAZE

1 tablespoon vegetable oil

2 garlic cloves, minced

3 tablespoons rice wine or dry sherry

1 cup *char siu* sauce

½ cup cider vinegar

2 tablespoons soy sauce

1½ teaspoons Chinese five-spice powder

Zest of 2 oranges, removed with a vegetable peeler and minced (2 tablespoons)

2 tablespoons Asian sesame oil

2 green onions, white and light green parts only, finely chopped (3 tablespoons)

SWEET-AND-SPICY RUB

½ cup firmly packed dark brown sugar

2 tablespoons kosher salt

1 tablespoon Chinese five-spice powder

1 teaspoon ground coriander

1 teaspoon cayenne pepper

7½ pounds pork spareribs

1 cup rice vinegar

3 cups apple wood chips, soaked in water to cover for 1 hour

To make the Five-Spice Glaze, in a saucepan over medium heat, heat the vegetable oil. Add the garlic and cook, stirring often, until it is fragrant and begins to brown, about 1 minute. Add the wine and cook until it evaporates. Stir in the *char siu* sauce, vinegar, soy sauce, five-spice powder, orange zest, and sesame oil and bring to a simmer for 2 minutes, stirring often. Remove from the heat and stir in the green onions. Transfer to a bowl and let cool completely. (The glaze can be made up to 1 day ahead, cooled, covered, and refrigerated.)

To make the Sweet-and-Spicy Rub, in a small bowl, combine the sugar, salt, five-spice powder, coriander, and cayenne and stir well.

Lay a slab of spareribs, bone side up, on a work surface. At one corner of the slab, using a small, sharp knife, nick the membrane that covers the bones. Grab the membrane with a kitchen towel and pull it off. (This may take a few attempts, but you'll get it.) Repeat with all of the rib slabs. Cut each slab in half crosswise. Massage the rub all over the ribs.

Prepare an indirect fire in a charcoal or gas grill (see Chef's Note, page 106). In a bowl, combine the vinegar with 1 cup water. Pour into a spray bottle and set aside.

Place a metal rib rack on the cooking grate over the foil pan. Stand the ribs in the rack. Add 2 cups water to the pan. Sprinkle a handful of drained chips over the coals, or sprinkle them in the smoker box of a gas grill. Cover and grill the ribs, spraying them with the vinegar mixture and adding a handful of drained chips to the fire or smoker box every 45 minutes, along with additional briquettes as needed, until the ribs are very tender and beginning to pull away from the bone, about 2½ hours. Transfer the ribs to a large platter and set aside.

To glaze the ribs, for a charcoal grill, add about 3 pounds briquettes to the coals and let burn until they are covered with white ash. Spread out the coals. For a gas grill, increase the heat to high.

continued >

Place the ribs, bone side up, directly on the cooking grate. Brush with some of the glaze, turn the ribs over, and brush the tops with the glaze. Grill until the glaze on the underside is bubbling and caramelized, about 2 minutes. Turn the ribs and grill until the second sides are glazed. Transfer the ribs to a carving board and let stand for 5 minutes.

Cut between the ribs, transfer the ribs to a platter, and serve.

CHEF'S NOTE: *Indirect grilling is used for foods that take a long time to cook through. Spareribs and whole turkeys are perfect examples of foods that require this technique. Soaked and drained wood chips are often added to the fire to provide smoky flavor. The idea is to maintain an interior grill temperature of about 300°F. Most gas grills have a thermometer in their lids, but for charcoal grills, drop a deep-frying thermometer with a long metal stem through the vent in the lid to get a temperature reading.*

To set up a charcoal grill for indirect cooking, build a fire on one side of the grill with about 3 pounds briquettes. Let the fire burn until the coals are covered with white ash. On the empty side of the grill, place a 9-by-13-inch disposable aluminum foil pan. For a gas grill, preheat one burner on high, and leave the other burners off. Place the foil pan on the turned-off side of the grill.

To add wood chips to the grill, soak the wood chips in cold water to cover for an hour or so. When you are ready to add them to the grill, grab a handful and let the water drain away. For a charcoal grill, sprinkle the chips directly on the coals. They will start smoldering and smoking almost immediately. For a gas grill, use a metal smoker box, available at hardware stores. Place the box directly on the heat source and let it get very hot. Sprinkle a handful of drained chips into the box and wait for them to smolder and smoke, which may take a few minutes.

GRILLED CHICKEN PIRI-PIRI

Piri-piri is an all-purpose West African hot sauce and marinade. It is authentically made with the tiny, very hot piri-piri chile, a type of bird's-eye chile, but the more readily available habanero (no slouch in the heat department itself) is an able substitute. Smoky and spicy, this grilled chicken will become a new favorite. [CHEF JONATHAN ROHLAND]

Serves 6

PIRI-PIRI MARINADE

¾ cup fresh lime juice

½ cup dry white wine

½ cup extra-virgin olive oil

8 cloves garlic, minced

2 tablespoons smoked paprika such as pimentón de la Vera

2 habanero chiles, seeded, deribbed, and minced

2 tablespoons peeled and minced fresh ginger

2 tablespoons finely chopped fresh flat-leaf parsley

2 tablespoons kosher salt

6 skin-on, bone-in chicken breast halves (10 ounces each)

1 teaspoon kosher salt

½ teaspoon freshly ground black pepper

Vegetable oil for the grill

To make the Piri-Piri Marinade, in a bowl, whisk together the lime juice, wine, oil, garlic, smoked paprika, chiles, ginger, parsley, and salt. Remove ½ cup of the marinade from the bowl, cover, and refrigerate it. It will be used for basting the chicken during grilling.

Place the chicken in a 1-gallon lock-top plastic bag, and pour the marinade over the chicken, coating it well. Squeeze all of the air out of the bag and seal it. Refrigerate at least 12 hours or up to 24 hours, turning the bag occasionally to distribute the flavors evenly.

Prepare a banked fire in a charcoal or gas grill (see Chef's Note).

Remove the chicken breasts from the marinade, and discard the marinade in the bag. Season the chicken lightly with the salt and pepper. Oil the cooking grate. Place the chicken breasts, skin side down, on the hotter area of the grill and cover. Grill until the undersides are seared with grill marks, about 3 minutes. Rotate the chicken 90 degrees to create attractive cross-hatching, brush with the reserved marinade, and grill for 3 minutes longer. Turn the chicken over and move to the cooler area of the grill. Continue grilling, occasionally brushing the chicken with the remaining marinade, until an instant-read thermometer inserted in the thickest part of a breast without touching the bone reads 170°F, about 30 minutes.

Transfer the chicken breasts to a platter and let rest for 5 minutes. Serve hot.

CHEF'S NOTE: *Banked grilling provides two cooking areas that are maintained at different temperatures. For a charcoal grill, build a fire with 5 pounds briquettes, and let it burn until the coals are covered with white ash. Using long tongs, bank the coals in a slope so that one side of the grill has a thicker layer of coals than the other. For a gas grill, preheat the grill on high, then leave one burner on high and turn the other burner(s) to low. You now have two grilling zones, one hot and the other cooler.*

CUBAN SMOKED PORK SHOULDER

Bursting with Caribbean flavors, this pork shoulder recipe delivers an unbelievably succulent result. The bitter-orange brine deeply seasons the meat, a spicy rub adds more complexity, the smoke does its work, and the whole dish is pulled together with an orange *mojo* sauce. It takes time to slowly cook this large cut to doneness, but it is time well spent. [RICHARD LADD]

Serves 8 to 10

1 bone-in pork picnic shoulder, with skin (about 7½ pounds)

ORANGE BRINE

4 cups fresh bitter orange juice (from about 16 bitter oranges, see Chef's Note)

¾ cup sugar

1½ cups kosher salt

2 large heads garlic, separated into cloves, peeled, and crushed

SPICE PASTE

12 cloves garlic, chopped

Grated zest of 2 large oranges (2 tablespoons)

3 tablespoons cider vinegar

3 tablespoons extra-virgin olive oil

2 tablespoons ground cumin

2 tablespoons dried oregano

2 tablespoons dried thyme

1 tablespoon granulated onion

1 tablespoon freshly ground black pepper

3 cups cherrywood chips, soaked in water to cover for 1 hour

Twenty-four hours before cooking, prepare and brine the pork shoulder. Using a paring knife, make 1-inch-deep slits, closely spaced, all over the roast.

To make the Orange Brine, in a deep plastic container large enough to hold the pork and brine, whisk together the bitter orange juice, sugar, and salt to dissolve the sugar and salt. Add the crushed garlic and the pork and cover the container. (Or, make the brine in a bowl, and combine the pork, garlic, and brine in a turkey-sized oven roasting bag. Add the brine to the bag, close the bag, and place it in a large bowl.) Refrigerate, occasionally turning the pork in the brine, for 24 hours.

To make the Spice Paste, in a bowl, combine the garlic, orange zest, vinegar, oil, cumin, oregano, thyme, granulated onion, and pepper and mix to form a paste. Drain the pork shoulder and rinse it under cold running water. Pat it dry with paper towels. Rub the pork all over with the spice paste, forcing some of the paste into the slits.

Prepare an indirect fire in a charcoal or gas grill (see Chef's Note, page 106).

Place the pork shoulder on the cooking grate over the foil pan. Add 2 cups water to the pan. Sprinkle a handful of drained chips over the coals, or sprinkle them in the smoker box of a gas grill. Cover and cook the pork shoulder, adding a handful of drained chips to the fire or smoker box every 45 minutes, until the pork is very tender when pierced with a meat fork and an instant-read thermometer inserted in the thickest part of the shoulder without touching bone reads 190°F, about 6 hours. For a charcoal grill, add 8 fresh briquettes to the coals along with the chips to maintain the heat at about 325°F. Transfer the pork to a carving board, tent with aluminum foil, and let rest for 45 minutes.

ORANGE MOJO

½ cup fresh orange juice (from 2 large navel or Valencia oranges)

½ cup cider vinegar

8 cloves garlic, finely chopped

1 tablespoon kosher salt

1 teaspoon ground cumin

1 teaspoon dried oregano

½ teaspoon freshly ground black pepper

1 cup extra-virgin olive oil

Meanwhile, make the Orange Mojo. In a bowl, whisk together the navel orange juice, vinegar, garlic, salt, cumin, oregano, and pepper. Gradually whisk in the oil to form an emulsion. Cover and set aside.

To carve, remove the skin in one piece. Scrape any excess fat off the skin and cut the skin into serving pieces. Cut the meat off the bone into 3 or 4 large pieces. Slice the meat across the grain. Arrange the slices on a serving platter, and top with the pieces of crisp skin. Drizzle with about ¼ cup of the *mojo* sauce. Serve hot, with any remaining sauce on the side.

CHEF'S NOTE: *Bitter (Seville) oranges can be found at Latin groceries. Bitter oranges contain less juice than sweet oranges, so plan on about ¼ cup juice from each orange. You might want to buy a few extra oranges to be sure you end up with enough juice. If you can't find bitter oranges, substitute 2 cups each fresh grapefruit juice and fresh navel or Valencia orange juice.*

TEQUILA CHICKEN SKEWERS
WITH PINEAPPLE MANGO CHUTNEY

This tequila marinade is great with chicken, but it also goes well with fish or shrimp. In this recipe, I'm threading skinless, boneless chicken breast meat onto bamboo skewers for serving as finger food at a cocktail party or reception. Try the marinade another time with bone-in chicken pieces. [CHEF JOE NOONAN]

Serves 6

TEQUILA MARINADE

¾ cup canola oil

¼ cup silver tequila

⅓ cup fresh lime juice

¼ cup lemon-lime carbonated beverage

¼ cup chopped fresh cilantro stems and leaves

1 jalapeño chile, including seeds and ribs, chopped

1 shallot, thinly sliced

2 cloves garlic, thinly sliced

2½ teaspoons kosher salt

½ teaspoon freshly ground black pepper

2½ pounds boneless, skinless chicken breasts

To make the Tequila Marinade, in a blender, combine the oil, tequila, lime juice, lemon-lime beverage, cilantro, jalapeño, shallot, garlic, salt, and pepper and process until smooth.

Holding the knife at a 45-degree angle, and cutting across the grain, cut the chicken into long pieces ¾ inch wide. Place the chicken in a 1-gallon lock-top plastic bag and pour in the marinade. Squeeze out all of the air and seal the bag. Refrigerate for at least 2 hours or up to 8 hours.

Meanwhile, make the Pineapple Mango Chutney. In a saucepan over medium heat, combine the vinegar, honey, and Worcestershire sauce and bring to a simmer. Stir in the pineapple and mango and bring to a boil. Reduce the heat to medium-low and simmer until the fruit is tender, about 20 minutes. Remove from the heat and let cool slightly, then stir in the bell pepper and cilantro. Transfer to a serving bowl and let cool completely.

Season the chutney to taste with salt and pepper. Transfer about two-thirds of the chutney to a food processor fitted with the metal chopping blade and pulse until just short of a purée. Return it to the bowl and stir to combine. Cover and refrigerate until ready to serve.

Remove the chicken from the marinade, and discard the marinade. Weave 3 or 4 of the chicken strips onto each of the skewers. Using a flat meat mallet, gently flatten the chicken strips.

PINEAPPLE MANGO CHUTNEY

1 cup red wine vinegar

½ cup honey

2 tablespoons Worcestershire sauce

2 cups cored and diced fresh
   pineapple (½-inch dice)

2 cups pitted, skinned, and diced
   ripe mango (½-inch dice)

1 red bell pepper, seeded, deribbed,
   and cut into ¼-inch dice

⅓ cup chopped fresh cilantro

½ teaspoon kosher salt

¼ teaspoon freshly ground black
   pepper

12 (10-inch) bamboo skewers,
   soaked in water to cover for
   2 hours and drained

Vegetable oil for the grill

Prepare a medium-hot fire in a charcoal grill, or preheat a gas grill on medium-high (see Chef's Note, page 126).

Lightly oil the cooking grate. Place the skewers on the grill and grill until the undersides are seared with grill marks, about 3 minutes. Turn the skewers over and grill until the chicken shows no sign of pink when pierced with the tip of a knife, about 3 minutes more.

Arrange the skewers on a platter and serve immediately. Pass the chutney at the table.

GRILLED CAPRESE PIZZA WITH ROSEMARY PARMESAN CRUST

Grilled pizza is now almost as popular as the traditional baked version. This recipe, with fresh tomatoes and basil on an herbed crust, evokes fond memories of friends and family around the grill, sharing good times and great food and drink. It is an especially refreshing start to an outdoor meal, or it makes a good main course for a light supper. To serve the pizzas at their piping-hot best, devour each one as it comes off the grill. You can also freeze half of the dough for another meal. [ERIC SALZER]

Serves 6

ROSEMARY PARMESAN DOUGH

1¼ cups warm (105° to 115°F) water

1 package (2¼ teaspoons) active dry yeast

1 teaspoon sugar

¼ cup extra-virgin olive oil, plus more for coating the bowl

2 teaspoons kosher salt

3½ cups unbleached all-purpose flour, or as needed

2 tablespoons freshly grated Parmesan cheese, preferably Parmigiano-Reggiano

1 tablespoon finely chopped fresh rosemary

TOPPING

3 tablespoons extra-virgin olive oil, plus more for brushing the pizzas

1 large yellow onion, thinly sliced

Kosher salt

Freshly cracked black pepper

5 plum tomatoes, cored, quartered lengthwise, and seeded

Olive oil for the grill

½ pound fresh mozzarella cheese, sliced about ³⁄₁₆ inch thick

¾ cup whole Simple Roasted Garlic cloves (page 61)

10 large fresh basil leaves, cut into fine ribbons

1½ tablespoons Balsamic Drizzle (page 176)

To make the Rosemary Parmesan Dough, pour the warm water into the bowl of a stand mixer fitted with the paddle attachment and sprinkle in the yeast and sugar. Let stand until foamy, about 5 minutes.

With the mixer on low speed, beat just until the yeast dissolves. Add the oil and salt and mix until combined. Add 3 cups of the flour, 1 cup at a time, mixing until incorporated after each addition. Add the Parmesan and rosemary and mix until combined. Continue adding enough of the remaining ½ cup flour to make a dough that pulls away from the sides of the bowl. Change to the dough hook, and increase the mixer speed to medium. Knead just until the dough is smooth and supple, about 5 minutes.

Turn the dough out onto a clean work surface (add flour to the surface only if the dough is sticking) and knead it by hand until it is elastic, about 2 minutes. Lightly coat a large bowl with oil. Place the dough in the bowl and turn the dough to coat it completely with oil. Cover the bowl with plastic wrap and let stand in a warm spot until the dough has doubled in volume, about 1¼ hours.

Punch down the dough, re-cover the bowl, and let rise again until doubled in volume, about 1 hour. (If you are in a hurry, you can skip the second rise, but the dough will not be as light.)

Meanwhile, make caramelized onions for the Topping. In a large nonstick skillet over medium heat, heat 2 tablespoons of the oil. Add the onion and cook, stirring often and adjusting the heat as needed so the onion cooks steadily without burning, until the onion is deep golden brown, about 15 minutes. Season to taste with salt and pepper. Transfer to a bowl and let cool.

To make the oven-roasted tomatoes for the Topping, preheat the oven to 375°F. In a bowl, toss the tomatoes with the remaining 1 tablespoon oil, and season with a little salt and pepper. Spread the tomatoes evenly, skin side up, on a rimmed baking sheet. Bake until tender, about 20 minutes. Transfer to another bowl and let cool.

Prepare a banked fire in a charcoal or gas grill (see Chef's Note, page 107). Have ready four 12-inch squares of parchment paper.

continued >

Turn the dough out onto a work surface and cut it into 4 equal pieces. Dust 1 parchment square with flour. Place 1 portion of the dough on the floured parchment. Cover the remaining dough with plastic wrap. Stretch and pat out the dough to form a 10-inch circle. If the dough retracts during stretching, cover it loosely with plastic wrap and let it stand for a few minutes to relax, then continue. Center the stretched dough on the floured parchment and cover the dough circle with plastic wrap. Repeat with the remaining dough pieces and parchment squares.

Lightly oil the cooking grate. Gently lift a dough circle and drape it onto the grate over the hotter area of the grill. Grill until the underside begins to crisp and toast to a light brown and the top begins to puff, about 1½ minutes. Using tongs and a wide spatula, slide the dough to the cooler area of the grill and cook until the underside is nicely browned, 3 to 5 minutes. Brush the uncooked top with oil.

Using the tongs and spatula, gently flip the crust back over the hotter area of the grill and grill until the underside is set and lightly browned, about 1 minute. Slide over to the cooler area and brush again with oil. Remove from the grill with the tongs and spatula and top with one-fourth each of the mozzarella, roasted garlic, roasted tomatoes, and caramelized onion. Return to the grill, cover, and grill until the cheese is melted, about 2 minutes. Using the tongs and spatula, slide the pizza onto a serving platter.

Sprinkle with the basil and drizzle with the glaze. Cut into wedges and serve hot. Make 3 more pizzas the same way with the remaining dough and topping ingredients.

CHEF'S NOTE: *The beauty of pizza is that you can create your own favorite version by using this recipe as a blueprint. You can also streamline the process by buying, rather than making, some of the ingredients, such as frozen pizza dough, roasted garlic or tomatoes, and even balsamic glaze.*

ANCHO PORK CHOPS WITH LIME DRIZZLE

Ancho chiles, with their slightly sweet flavor profile, are a terrific match for pork.
This southwestern barbecue gets much of its flavor from the grill, and is complemented by the fragrant lime drizzle.
Serve with plenty of hot tortillas and corn on the cob. [CHEF ALYSSA KASPAREK]

Serves 8

ANCHO RUB

1 ancho chile, seeded, deribbed, and torn into 6 or 7 pieces

1 tablespoon chili powder

1 teaspoon ground coriander

1½ teaspoons firmly packed brown sugar

2 teaspoons kosher salt

¾ teaspoon ground cumin

1 teaspoon dried oregano

1 teaspoon garlic powder

½ teaspoon sweet paprika, preferably Hungarian

Pinch of ground cinnamon

LIME DRIZZLE

¼ cup red wine vinegar

¼ cup fresh lime juice

2 tablespoons honey

⅓ cup extra-virgin olive oil

½ cup finely chopped fresh cilantro leaves

1 jalapeño chile, seeded, deribbed, and minced

2 cloves garlic, minced

1 teaspoon kosher salt

½ teaspoon freshly ground black pepper

8 center-cut loin pork chops (½ pound each)

Vegetable oil for the grill

To make the Ancho Rub, heat a large, heavy skillet over medium-high heat. Add the ancho chile pieces and cook, shaking the pan often, until they turn a darker shade and smell fragrant, about 3 minutes. Do not overcook. Transfer to a plate and let cool.

Using a spice grinder or blender, grind the cooled ancho pieces to a powder. Pour the ground chile into a small bowl. Add the chili powder, coriander, brown sugar, salt, cumin, oregano, garlic powder, paprika, and cinnamon and mix well. Set aside.

To make the Lime Drizzle, in a bowl, whisk together the vinegar, lime juice, and honey until combined. Gradually whisk in the oil. Whisk in the cilantro, jalapeño, garlic, salt, and pepper. Set aside.

French the chops: Using a thin-bladed, sharp knife, trim the meat and fat off of the bone of each chop until you reach its meaty "eye." (Removing the fatty meat and gristle helps the chops cook more evenly.) Massage the rub all over the pork chops. Set aside.

Prepare a banked fire in a charcoal or gas grill (see Chef's Note, page 107).

Lightly oil the cooking grate. Place the pork chops over the hotter area of the grill. Cover and grill until the undersides are seared with grill marks, about 2 minutes. Turn the chops and grill until seared with grill marks on the second sides, about 2 minutes more. Move the chops to the cooler area of the grill, re-cover, and cook until an instant-read thermometer inserted horizontally into the center of a chop without touching bone reads 140°F, about 10 minutes. Transfer the chops to a serving platter, arranging them in a shingled row, and let rest for 5 minutes.

Spoon the lime drizzle over the chops and serve immediately.

TOMATO AND GRILLED BREAD SALAD

One of my close friends, Peggy Peattie, is a renowned photographer who often photographs my food. Peggy is a vegetarian, so it is no surprise that my vegetable-based recipes are her favorite photography work. She relishes this dish for its colorful eye appeal, but more important, she loves the burst of flavors. The idea here is to take advantage of the many different kinds of tomatoes in the summer market, so mix whatever sizes and shapes strike your fancy. The grilled bread adds a crunchy contrast and a welcome hint of smokiness. [CHEF KIMBERLY HAZARD]

Serves 6

HERBED OIL

¾ cup extra-virgin olive oil

3 tablespoons finely chopped fresh basil

2 tablespoons finely chopped fresh oregano

2 tablespoons finely chopped fresh flat-leaf parsley

2 cloves garlic, chopped

1 tablespoon kosher salt

½ teaspoon freshly ground black pepper

SHERRY VINAIGRETTE

½ cup sherry vinegar

2 tablespoons chopped shallot

2 teaspoons sugar

2 teaspoons kosher salt

½ teaspoon freshly ground black pepper

¼ cup Herbed Oil

1 rustic-style sourdough baguette (1 pound), sliced ¾ inch thick

2 pounds assorted tomatoes such as heirloom, beefsteak, cherry, and teardrop, in various sizes and colors

½ pound fresh small mozzarella balls (*bocconcini*), drained and halved

10 large fresh basil leaves, torn into stamp-sized pieces

To make the Herbed Oil, in a bowl, stir together the oil, basil, oregano, parsley, garlic, salt, and pepper, mixing well. Measure ¼ cup of the herbed oil, and set both portions aside.

To make the Sherry Vinaigrette, in a bowl, whisk together the vinegar, shallot, sugar, salt, and pepper. Gradually whisk in the larger portion of herbed oil to form an emulsion. Set aside.

Prepare a hot fire in a charcoal grill, or preheat a charcoal grill on high (see Chef's Note, page 127).

Lightly brush both sides of the baguette slices with the reserved ¼ cup herbed oil. Place the slices on the grill and grill, turning as needed, until the slices are well toasted and lightly charred on both sides, about 1 minute total. Transfer to a platter and let cool completely. Tear the bread into bite-sized pieces.

Core the larger tomatoes and cut them into wedges. Core the smaller tomatoes and cut them in half.

In a large bowl, combine the tomatoes, mozzarella, and bread. Drizzle with the vinaigrette, add the basil, and toss gently. Taste and adjust the seasoning with salt and pepper. Serve at once.

HERB-GRILLED VEGETABLE SALAD WITH GOAT CHEESE

The secret to an amazing taste experience is to understand the layering of flavors. The components of this grilled salad—the vinaigrette, the variety of vegetables, the tangy goat cheese—are all there for a reason. The preparation steps are not difficult, and the result will be a gorgeous platter of grilled vegetables that sing out with the taste of summer. [CHEF JONAH MERRELL]

Serves 6

ROASTED-TOMATO VINAIGRETTE

3 plum tomatoes, cored and halved

½ cup plus 1 tablespoon extra-virgin olive oil, plus more for the pan

Kosher salt

Freshly ground black pepper

1 tablespoon balsamic vinegar

2 tablespoons sherry vinegar

4 large fresh basil leaves, chopped

2 tablespoons chopped shallot

1 tablespoon fresh thyme leaves

1 clove garlic, minced

1 pound jumbo asparagus, woody stem ends removed

1 large zucchini, ends trimmed, quartered lengthwise, and seeds removed

1 large yellow squash, ends trimmed, quartered lengthwise, and seeds removed

1 large red onion, cut crosswise into ¼-inch-thick slices and separated into rings

2 large portobello mushrooms, stems removed and dark gills scraped out with the tip of a spoon

1 large red bell pepper, seeded, deribbed, and cut lengthwise into sixths

⅓ cup extra-virgin olive oil, plus more for the grill

To make the Roasted-Tomato Vinaigrette, preheat the oven to 500°F. Oil a rimmed baking sheet.

In a bowl, toss the tomatoes with 1 tablespoon of the oil, ¼ teaspoon salt, and a pinch of pepper. Spread the tomatoes, skin side up, on the prepared baking sheet. Roast until the skin is deeply browned and somewhat charred, about 12 minutes. Let cool.

Remove the seeds from the tomatoes. In a blender, combine the tomatoes, balsamic and sherry vinegars, basil, shallot, thyme, and garlic and process until smooth, about 1 minute. With the machine running, add the remaining ½ cup oil in a thin, steady stream to form an emulsion. Season to taste with salt and pepper. Set aside.

Place the asparagus, zucchini, yellow squash, onion, mushrooms, and bell pepper in a large roasting pan. Drizzle with the oil and sprinkle with the rosemary, parsley, thyme, and garlic. Season with the salt and pepper and toss gently to coat. Set aside for 30 minutes.

Prepare a hot fire in a charcoal grill, or preheat a gas grill on high (see Chef's Note, page 127).

Lightly oil the cooking grate. Place the vegetables on the grill, with the pepper wedges skin side down. Grill until the undersides are seared with grill marks, about 3 minutes. Turn the vegetables over (leave the peppers skin side down) and grill until they are crisp-tender, 2 to 3 minutes more. Transfer to a large platter. Let cool to room temperature.

continued >

1 tablespoon fresh rosemary leaves

1½ tablespoons fresh flat-leaf
  parsley leaves

2 teaspoons fresh thyme leaves

1 clove garlic, minced

2 teaspoons kosher salt

¼ teaspoon freshly ground black
  pepper

6 ounces mesclun (mixed baby salad
  greens)

6 ounces fresh goat cheese,
  crumbled

Remove the blistered skins from the pepper wedges. Cut all of the vegetables into bite-sized pieces.

In a large bowl, toss the vegetables with the vinaigrette, and season to taste with salt and pepper. Add the mesclun and gently toss again.

Divide the salad among dinner plates, sprinkle evenly with the goat cheese, and serve.

CILANTRO LIME GRILLED SHRIMP

This simple recipe produces spectacular results every time. The shrimp can be somewhat messy to eat
because they are grilled and served in their shells, but I have always found that cooking shrimp with their shells intact
results in superior taste and texture. [CHEF MICHAEL NORTHERN]

Serves 6

2 pounds extra-large (16/20 count)
shrimp in the shell (see Chef's
Note, page 142)

CILANTRO LIME MARINADE

¼ cup seasoned rice vinegar

⅓ cup fresh lime juice

⅓ cup honey, preferably clover

¾ cup firmly packed chopped fresh
cilantro stems and leaves

1 tablespoon *sambal oelek*

3 large cloves garlic, minced

1 teaspoon kosher salt

¼ teaspoon freshly ground black
pepper

⅓ cup canola oil

6 (10-inch) bamboo skewers, soaked
in water to cover for 2 hours and
drained

Vegetable oil for the grill

Using a paring knife, split the shell of each shrimp along the back (concave side), leaving the
tail segments intact. Lift out the vein with the tip of the knife or your fingers. Place the shrimp
in a bowl and set aside.

To make the Cilantro Lime Marinade, in a bowl, whisk together the vinegar, lime juice, honey,
cilantro, *sambal oelek,* garlic, salt, pepper, and oil. Remove ⅓ cup of the marinade to use as
a final glaze for the shrimp. Pour the remaining marinade over the shrimp and toss to coat
evenly. Cover and refrigerate for at least 30 minutes or up to 2 hours.

Remove the shrimp from the marinade and discard the marinade. Thread the shrimp onto
the skewers, piercing each shrimp through the tail and again through the meaty portion.

Prepare a medium-hot fire in a charcoal grill, or preheat a gas grill on medium-high (see
Chef's Note, page 126).

Lightly oil the cooking grate. Place the skewers on the grill and grill until the undersides are
seared with grill marks, 2 to 3 minutes. Turn the skewers over and grill until the shrimp are
opaque, 2 to 3 minutes more.

Using tongs, transfer the skewers to warmed dinner plates or a large platter. Remove the
skewers. Baste the shrimp with the reserved ⅓ cup marinade. Serve immediately.

CHEF'S NOTE: *The finest shrimp I have ever cooked are white shrimp in the shell, caught off of
Mexico's west coast. Farm–raised white shrimp pale in comparison.*

LONE STAR RIB-EYE STEAK

When I relocated to Dallas, I was told that everything in Texas was big. I didn't believe it until one day a meat vendor brought in a rib-eye steak that weighed in at 1¼ pounds! To re-create this steak (sometimes called a cowboy steak or tomahawk steak), ask your butcher to cut individual bone-in rib chops from a rib roast, with the bones frenched to the eye of the meat. Don't try to rush this steak. Its size means that it will take more time than the typical thinner cuts. [CHEF RICHARD SILVA]

Serves 4

4 bone-in rib-eye chops, cut
   1¼ inches thick (1¼ pounds each)

1½ tablespoons Southwestern
   Seasoning (page 41)

Vegetable oil for the grill

4 tablespoons Garlic Herb Butter
   (page 77)

Season the steaks on both sides with the Southwestern Seasoning. Wrap the exposed bones with aluminum foil to prevent charring. Cover loosely with plastic wrap and let stand at room temperature for 1 hour.

Prepare a banked fire in a charcoal or gas grill (see Chef's Note, page 107).

Lightly oil the cooking grate. Place the steaks over the hotter area of the grill. Cover and grill until the undersides are seared with grill marks, about 2 minutes. Rotate the steaks 90 degrees to create attractive cross-hatching, re-cover, and grill for 2 minutes more. Turn the steaks over, and repeat the searing on the second sides, about 4 minutes total. Move the steaks to the cooler area of the grill. Cover and grill, turning occasionally, until an instant-read thermometer inserted horizontally through the side of the steak into the center without touching bone reads 130°F for medium-rare, about 15 minutes.

Transfer the steaks, with the hottest side up, to 4 warmed dinner plates. Top each steak with 1 tablespoon of the herb butter and serve immediately.

GRILLED DIVER SCALLOPS
WITH ROASTED-TOMATO BUTTER SAUCE

Scallops are delicate and easy to overcook. To ensure you end up with moist, plump grilled scallops, buy very large (U-10, for "under 10 to the pound") diver scallops and give them a gentle poaching before they hit the grill. Here, they are touched with the essence of apple smoke and then further enhanced by a delicate beurre blanc. Time the sauce so it is finished just before you grill the scallops. It will stay warm for the few minutes they cook. Or, make it up to an hour ahead and store it in a widemouthed vacuum jar. In the warmer months, serve the scallops with a citrus-marinated fennel salad; in cool weather, accompany them with a creamy risotto. [CHEF JONAH MERRELL]

Serves 4

12 very large (U-10) diver sea scallops (about 1¼ pounds total), tough small side muscles removed

ROASTED-TOMATO PURÉE

2 tablespoons extra-virgin olive oil, plus more for the pan

2 plum tomatoes, cored, seeded, and halved

1 teaspoon kosher salt

¼ teaspoon freshly ground black pepper

1 tablespoon minced shallot

2 cloves garlic, chopped

1 tablespoon chopped fresh thyme

1 tablespoon balsamic vinegar

1 teaspoon sherry vinegar

BEURRE BLANC

1 cup dry white wine

1 shallot, thinly sliced into half-moons

½ teaspoon black peppercorns

1 bay leaf

6 fresh thyme sprigs

Kosher salt

3 tablespoons heavy (whipping) cream

In a large saucepan, combine the scallops with water to cover by 1 inch. Bring to a bare simmer over medium-high heat, cover, and immediately remove from the heat. Let stand for 5 minutes. Carefully pour off the water and add cold water to the pan to stop the cooking. Drain the scallops in a colander, and pat dry with paper towels. Cover and refrigerate until ready to grill.

To make the Roasted-Tomato Purée, preheat the oven to 500°F. Oil a large rimmed baking sheet.

In a small bowl, toss together the tomatoes, oil, salt, and pepper. Spread evenly, skin side up, on the prepared baking sheet. Roast until the skins are deeply browned and somewhat charred, about 12 minutes. Remove from the oven, let cool, and remove the skins.

In a blender, combine the tomatoes, shallot, garlic, thyme, and the balsamic and sherry vinegars and process to a purée. Transfer to a bowl.

Prepare a medium-hot fire in a charcoal grill, or preheat a gas grill on medium (see Chef's Note, page 126). While the grill heats, brush the cooking grate a few times with vegetable oil. (This will help prevent the scallops from sticking.)

To make the Beurre Blanc, in a saucepan over high heat, combine the wine, shallot, peppercorns, bay leaf, thyme, and ½ teaspoon salt and bring to a boil. Reduce the heat to medium and cook at a brisk simmer until the liquid is almost evaporated, about 10 minutes. Add the cream and boil until reduced to 1 tablespoon. Remove the pan from the heat, and then adjust the heat to very low. Whisk in the butter, 1 cube at a time, allowing it to soften into a creamy sauce without melting and occasionally returning the pan to the low heat for a few seconds. When the butter has been incorporated, whisk in the lemon juice. Strain through a fine-mesh sieve into a small saucepan. Stir in the tomato purée and season to taste with salt. Keep the sauce in a warm spot on the stove for up to 15 minutes. Be careful not to overheat the sauce or it will curdle. The sauce is not served piping hot, but is instead heated by the temperature of the food it accompanies.

continued >

½ cup (1 stick) unsalted butter, cut into ½-inch cubes, at room temperature

1 teaspoon fresh lemon juice

1 teaspoon kosher salt

1 cup apple wood chips, soaked in water to cover for 1 hour

Vegetable oil for brushing the scallops and the grill

½ teaspoon freshly ground black pepper

For a charcoal grill, drain the chips and sprinkle them over the coals. For a gas grill, drain the chips, put them in a smoker box directly on the heat source, and let the chips smolder until they give off smoke, about 10 minutes.

Lightly oil the scallops and season them on all sides with the salt and pepper. Place on the grill, cover, and grill until the undersides are seared with grill marks, about 1 minute. Rotate the scallops 45 degrees to create attractive cross-hatching and cook for about 1 minute more. Turn the scallops over and repeat the searing on the second sides for 2 minutes more for medium-rare scallops.

To serve, arrange 3 scallops in the center of each warmed dinner plate. Spoon an equal amount of the beurre blanc around and over the scallops. Serve immediately.

CHEF'S NOTE: *A medium-hot fire is useful for foods that cook best over moderate heat, such as poultry and seafood. For a charcoal grill, build a fire with about 5 pounds briquettes, and let it burn until the coals are covered with white ash. Spread out the coals in an even layer, leaving a 2-inch border around the perimeter. Let the coals burn down until you can hold your hand 1 inch above the cooking grate for about 3 seconds. If the fat in the food drips onto the coals and causes excessive flare-ups, move the food to the perimeter of the grate where the fat will drip around, not onto, the coals. On a gas grill, adjust the thermostat so the temperature is about 400°F.*

GRILLED SKIRT STEAK WITH CHIMICHURRI

When I traveled to South America, I spent some time with a family in the Argentine countryside.
I had one of my most memorable meals there: a variety of grilled meats cooked over an open flame. The meats were marinated
in *chimichurri* sauce, a traditional Argentine accompaniment to red meat. Serve this steak with grilled vegetables like zucchini
and corn on the cob, and pour a Rioja at the table. [CHEF CORY GOODMAN]

Serves 6

CHIMICHURRI

1½ cups chopped fresh flat-leaf
    parsley

1 cup extra-virgin olive oil

½ cup chopped fresh cilantro

¼ cup cider vinegar

¼ cup chopped garlic

3 green onions, white and light
    green parts only, sliced

2 teaspoons red pepper flakes

2 tablespoons fresh lime juice

1 tablespoon kosher salt

2 teaspoons freshly ground black
    pepper

2½ pounds skirt steak, cut into 2 or
    3 portions, trimmed of excess fat

2 teaspoons kosher salt

1 teaspoon freshly ground black
    pepper

To make the Chimichurri, in a large bowl, whisk together the parsley, oil, cilantro, vinegar, garlic, green onions, red pepper flakes, lime juice, salt, and pepper. Remove ¾ cup of the mixture, cover, and refrigerate. It will be served as a sauce with the steak.

Place the steak in a 1-gallon lock-top plastic bag. Pour the remaining *chimichurri* over the steak. Squeeze all of the air out of the bag and seal it. Refrigerate for at least 12 hours or up to 24 hours, turning the bag occasionally to distribute the flavors evenly.

Prepare a hot fire in a charcoal grill, or preheat a gas grill on high (see Chef's Note).

Remove the pieces of steak from the bag, draining well, and discard the marinade. Season the steak with the salt and pepper. Place the steak on the grill, cover, and cook for about 5 minutes. Flip the steak over, re-cover, and continue cooking until cooked to desired temperature, 6 to 7 minutes more for medium. Transfer to a carving board, tent with aluminum foil, and let rest for about 10 minutes.

Just before carving, brush the steak with some of the reserved *chimichurri*. With the knife held at a 45-degree angle, cut the steak into thin slices across the grain. Place on a warmed serving platter or dinner plates. Serve immediately. Pass the remaining *chimichurri* at the table.

CHEF'S NOTE: *A hot fire should be reserved for grilling thin foods that will sear and cook fairly quickly. For a charcoal grill, build a fire with about 5 pounds briquettes, and let the coals burn until they are covered with white ash. Leave the coals heaped in a mound in the center of the grill. This gives you a cool perimeter around the coals where you can move the food if it drips fat that causes flare-ups. You should be able to hold your hand 1 inch above the cooking grate for only a second or two. For a gas grill, preheat the grill on high, allowing at least 15 minutes to heat thoroughly.*

APPLE WOOD–SMOKED LOBSTER

Even though it has been twenty years since I first tasted this dish, I still remember its simplicity and its elegant flavors.
Paired with well-chilled Champagne and served with clarified butter for dipping, the succulent lobster affords a luxury that you and
your guests will not soon forget. This recipe calls for spiny Florida lobster, but it also can be made with Maine lobster. Spiny lobster,
although related to the American lobster, has no claws. The tail contains more meat than the tail of its cousin,
and the flesh is sweeter and less prone to toughness or chewiness.   [CHEF MICHAEL NORTHERN]

Serves 4

1 cup (2 sticks) unsalted butter

2 cups apple wood chips, soaked in water to cover for 1 hour

2 lobsters, preferably spiny lobsters, (or 4 rock lobster tails, thawed) split in half lengthwise and tails held straight with a metal skewer

Prepare an indirect fire in a charcoal or gas grill (see Chef's Note, page 106).

Meanwhile, clarify the butter. In a small saucepan over medium-low heat, allow the butter to melt slowly. When it has fully melted, remove the pan from the heat and let stand for a few minutes. Skim off and discard any solids floating on the surface. Spoon or carefully ladle off the clear yellow portion—this is the clarified butter—and then discard the milky sediment that remains in the bottom of the pan. Set aside at room temperature. If the butter solidifies, reheat it gently over low heat.

For a charcoal grill, drain the chips and sprinkle them over the coals. For a gas grill, drain the chips, put them in a smoker box directly on the heat source, and let the chips smolder until they give off smoke, about 10 minutes.

Place the lobsters, shell side up, on the cooking grate over the foil pan and cover. In a charcoal grill, open the top and bottom vents to their widest position. Grill the lobsters until their exposed flesh begins to lose its translucence, about 6 minutes. Using long tongs, carefully flip the lobsters over. Re-cover and grill until the flesh is opaque, about 7 minutes more.

Serve the lobsters hot from the grill with individual dishes of clarified butter for dipping.

CHEF'S NOTE: *Apple wood chips give off a sweet, fruity smoke that accentuates many foods, especially seafood. They are more versatile than mesquite or hickory chips, both of which can generate smoke that is quite strong. Look for apple wood chips at hardware stores or online.*

OCEAN

BISTRO CRAB STACK

When I was cooking in San Diego, salads and light dishes were the most popular items on the menu,
forcing me to create new specials to meet the demand. This colorful composed salad, stacked in successive layers,
will make you look like a star chef at any gathering. You will need four short lengths of PVC pipe to help mold the stacks.
While metal molds are available at some professional-kitchen supply shops, you can have the PVC pipes cut to order
at your local hardware superstore. [CHEF RICHARD SILVA]

Serves 4

1 ripe avocado, halved, pitted, peeled, and cut into ¼-inch dice (about ¾ cup)

About ¾ cup Cilantro Lime Vinaigrette (page 84)

1 ripe tomato, cored, seeded, and cut into ¼-inch dice (about ¾ cup)

¼ seedless (English) cucumber, halved lengthwise, any tiny seeds removed, and cut into ¼-inch dice (about ¾ cup)

½ ripe mango, peeled, pitted, and cut into ¼-inch dice (about ¾ cup)

½ pound jumbo lump crabmeat, picked over for shell bits

2 tablespoons microgreens or finely chopped fresh chives

You need 4 pieces of PVC pipe each 3 inches in diameter and 4 inches long. Stand 1 piece in the center of each of 4 serving plates.

In a small bowl, gently toss the avocado with 2 tablespoons of the vinaigrette. Divide the avocado evenly among the molds, gently pressing it into the bottom of each mold to create a thin layer. Place the tomato, cucumber, and mango in 3 separate small bowls. Add 2 tablespoons of the vinaigrette to each bowl and toss gently. Divide the tomato, cucumber, and mango, in that order, evenly among the molds, gently pressing after each addition to create colorful layered stacks.

Divide the crabmeat (do not dress with the vinaigrette) among the molds, layering it on top. Carefully pull the molds up and away. Drizzle the remaining vinaigrette around each stack and sprinkle the greens on the stacks. Serve immediately.

CHAMPAGNE-STEAMED MUSSELS

Like many cooks, I have tried a number of different liquids for cooking mussels. White wine, beer, tomato juice, and even plain water have each been given their chance in the pot. But once I tried Champagne, there was no turning back, as the sparkling wine significantly deepens the fragrance and flavor of the shellfish. For the best results, use Prince Edward Island (PEI) mussels, but any premium quality mussel will do. [CHEF MICHAEL LYLE]

Serves 4

2 pounds Prince Edward Island mussels (about 4 dozen)

¼ cup extra-virgin olive oil

4 cloves garlic, thinly sliced

1 tablespoon finely chopped shallot

½ teaspoon red pepper flakes

2½ cups dry Champagne

2 tablespoons chopped fresh flat-leaf parsley

4 tablespoons (½ stick) unsalted butter, cut into cubes

Kosher salt

Freshly ground black pepper

Rinse the mussels under cold running water, and scrub them with a brush or new sponge. Discard any open mussels that don't close when rapped. Set aside.

In a large Dutch oven over low heat, heat the oil. Add the garlic and cook, stirring, until softened, about 1 minute. Stir in the shallot and red pepper flakes and cook, stirring often, until the garlic is golden, about 1 minute more.

Increase the heat to high and add the mussels, Champagne, and parsley. Cover tightly and bring to a boil. Cook, occasionally shaking the pot, until all of the mussel shells have opened, about 5 minutes. Remove from the heat.

Add the butter, re-cover, and swirl the pot until the butter has melted. Uncover and discard any unopened mussels. Season the broth generously with salt and pepper, keeping in mind that the broth will not cling to the mussels and needs to be flavorful.

Divide the mussels and broth among warmed deep bowls. Serve immediately.

CHEF'S NOTE: *Mussels from the cold Atlantic waters around Canada's Prince Edward Island are cultivated, not wild. They are especially plump and flavorful, and are without grit or tough beards that must be removed. If you use wild mussels, soak them in ice-cold water with a couple of table-spoons of cornmeal for 1 hour to help the shellfish expel any grit. Drain and scrub the mussels, and then, using pliers, pull out any tough beards, yanking them firmly toward the hinge.*

CRAB FRESCO WITH ANGEL HAIR PASTA

The key ingredients in this dish are browned garlic, tomato, butter, and jumbo lump crabmeat.
Together they are a wonderful complement to the delicate angel hair pasta. The final addition of spinach and shaved
Parmesan adds to a light and refreshing dish for any time of the year. [CHEF MICHAEL PALESH]

Serves 6

⅓ cup extra-virgin olive oil

¼ cup finely chopped garlic

¾ cup dry white wine

1 pound jumbo lump crabmeat,
    picked over for shell bits

1½ pints cherry or grape tomatoes,
    cored and halved lengthwise

1 cup (2 sticks) unsalted butter,
    at room temperature

4 cups firmly packed baby spinach

Kosher salt

Freshly ground black pepper

1 pound angel hair pasta

1 chunk (about 6 ounces) Parmesan
    cheese, preferably Parmigiano-
    Reggiano

12 fresh basil leaves

Bring a large pot of lightly salted water to a boil over high heat.

Meanwhile, in a large skillet over medium-high heat, heat the oil. Add the garlic and cook, stirring constantly, until it turns tan, about 1 minute. Stir in the wine (this stops the garlic from further browning) and cook for 1 minute to reduce by about half. Add the crabmeat and cook for 30 seconds. Add the tomatoes and cook, stirring often, until they give off their juices and the juices are reduced by half, about 4 minutes.

Reduce the heat to very low. Fold in the butter, a few tablespoons at a time, until incorporated (it should soften and melt without separating), about 2 minutes. Stir in the spinach and cook until it wilts, about 1 minute more. Season to taste with salt and pepper. Remove from the heat and cover to keep warm.

Add the pasta to the boiling water and cook until al dente, according to the package instructions. Drain in a colander, and then return the pasta to the warm cooking pot.

Add about half of the crab sauce to the pasta and toss gently. Season again with salt and pepper. Divide the pasta evenly among warmed bowls. Top the servings evenly with the remaining crab sauce. Using a vegetable peeler, shave curls of the Parmesan over each serving, and then garnish each serving with 2 basil leaves. Serve immediately.

CHEF'S NOTE: *Do not rinse pasta after draining. It will remove the starch that helps the sauce cling to the pasta. The only times rinsing is recommended are when cooking pasta for a salad and when cooking pasta a few hours ahead for finishing later.*

HUNAN HALIBUT WITH LEMON AND GREEN ONIONS

Asian cooks understand the interplay of sour, sweet, hot, and salty, as the ingredients in this savory dish illustrate: lemon, sugar, chiles, and oyster sauce each represent a flavor category. Pass chile oil at the table for guests who like their food spicy hot. [ERIC SALZER]

Serves 4

4 large dried shiitake mushrooms

1 lemon

5 green onions

4 quarter-sized rounds peeled fresh ginger, cut into julienne (3 tablespoons)

2 red jalapeño or serrano chiles, seeded, deribbed, and cut into julienne (3 tablespoons)

2 cloves garlic, minced

SAUCE

1 cup low-sodium chicken broth

2 tablespoons oyster sauce

1 teaspoon kosher salt

1 tablespoon sugar

1½ pounds halibut fillet, skinned and cut into four 4-inch squares

1 teaspoon Asian sesame oil

¾ teaspoon kosher salt

3 tablespoons peanut or vegetable oil

2 tablespoons rice wine or dry sherry

Hot steamed jasmine rice for serving

Place the dried mushrooms in a bowl and add hot water to cover. Let stand until softened, about 20 minutes. Drain, cut off and discard the stems, and cut the caps into julienne.

Using a vegetable peeler, remove the zest from the lemon. Cut the zest into very fine julienne about 2 inches in length. Squeeze the juice from the lemon, reserve 2 tablespoons, and save the remainder for another use.

Cut the white part of the green onions into 2-inch-long julienne; you should have ½ cup. Cut the green parts of the green onions into 2-inch-long julienne; you should have 1 cup. Place all of the julienned green onions in a bowl and add the mushroom caps, lemon zest, ginger, chiles, and garlic; set aside.

To make the Sauce, in a bowl, combine the broth, oyster sauce, salt, and sugar and mix well; set aside.

Rub the fish on both sides with the sesame oil, and season on both sides with the salt. Let stand at room temperature for at least 15 minutes or up to 30 minutes.

Heat a wok or large skillet over high heat until very hot. Add the peanut oil and heat until very hot but not smoking. Add the halibut pieces and cook until the undersides are beginning to brown, about 1 minute. Turn the fish pieces over, and move them to one side of the wok. Add the mushroom mixture to the empty area of the wok and stir-fry until the mixture is fragrant, about 30 seconds. Stir the sauce mixture, pour into the wok, and bring to a boil. Reduce the heat to medium and cook until the fish looks barely opaque when flaked in the center, about 3 minutes.

Using a slotted spatula, transfer each fish fillet to a warmed shallow bowl. Stir the wine into the vegetable mixture, and then add the reserved lemon juice. Using a slotted spoon, place an equal amount of the vegetables on each fillet. Pour equal amounts of the broth into each bowl. Serve hot, with the rice passed on the side.

CHEF'S NOTE: *When cutting several ingredients into julienne for the same dish, try to cut them into the same size to give the dish a tailored look. In this dish, julienned mushrooms, green onions, lemon, ginger, and chile should all be the same width and about the same length. The mushrooms and white part of the green onions may need to be cut in half before you cut them into julienne.*

HONEY AND GINGER-GLAZED SALMON

Chefs often borrow ideas, and this one came when my wife and I were vacationing in San Francisco.
It is simple to prepare, yet elegant to eat. Serve the salmon with steamed asparagus and buttered rice. [CHEF MICHAEL LYLE]

Serves 4

½ cup low-sodium soy sauce

4 skinless salmon fillets (6 ounces each)

3 tablespoons canola oil, plus more for the pan

1 teaspoon kosher salt

½ teaspoon freshly ground black pepper

3 tablespoons honey

1½ tablespoons peeled and very finely minced ginger

6 green onions, white and light green parts only, trimmed and finely chopped (¾ cup)

Pour the soy sauce into a wide, shallow dish. Add the salmon, skinned side up (the soy sauce should come only about halfway up the sides of the salmon). Cover with plastic wrap and refrigerate for 30 minutes, no longer. Remove the salmon from the soy sauce and pat dry with paper towels; discard the soy sauce.

Preheat the oven to 350° F. Lightly oil a rimmed baking sheet.

Season the salmon on both sides with the salt and pepper. In a small bowl, stir together the honey and ginger. Spread the green onions in another shallow dish. One fillet at a time, spread about 1½ teaspoons of the honey mixture over the marinated side of the salmon. Sprinkle about one-fourth of the green onions evenly over the honey, and press gently to adhere to the salmon. Transfer to a platter, green onion side up.

In a large nonstick skillet over medium heat, heat the oil until very hot but not smoking. Add the salmon fillets, green onion side down, and cook until the undersides are seared, about 1½ minutes. Transfer the salmon, onion side up, to the baking sheet. Roast until the salmon is barely opaque when flaked with the tip of a knife, about 10 minutes.

Using a thin, flexible metal spatula, transfer the salmon portions to warmed dinner plates. Serve immediately.

CHEF'S NOTE: *Salmon comes in several varieties, from king to coho, and you can find wild salmon at various times of the year. Salmon caught in colder waters, such as sockeye, will have more fatty layers, which give the fish the richest flavor. They will also have the best health benefits, thanks to their high concentration of omega-3 fatty acids.*

GRILLED MAHIMAHI WITH WHITE BEANS AND TOMATOES

Mahimahi is a firm fish that takes well to grilling. It also has a meaty flavor and texture than can stand up to
the flavor-packed white beans. Try this same cooking technique with other grill-friendly fish, such as salmon or red snapper.
For the best flavors, make this dish in the summertime when both tomato and
basil season are in full swing. [FARIS ZOMA]

Serves 4

WHITE BEANS AND TOMATOES

¼ cup extra-virgin olive oil

6 cloves garlic, minced

1 can (15 ounces) Great Northern
beans, rinsed and drained

2 ripe, large fresh tomatoes, cored,
seeded, and cut into ½-inch dice
(2 cups)

¼ cup finely chopped green onions
(white and light green parts only)

½ cup dry white wine

1 can (28 ounces) whole Italian-style
tomatoes in juice, preferably San
Marzano, drained and quartered

¼ cup chopped fresh basil

Kosher salt

Freshly ground black pepper

Vegetable oil for brushing the fish
and grill

4 skinless mahimahi fillets
(6 ounces each)

Extra-virgin olive oil for garnish

Fresh whole basil leaves for garnish

Prepare a medium-hot fire in a charcoal grill, or preheat a gas grill on medium (see Chef's Note, page 126).

To make the White Beans and Tomatoes, in a saucepan over medium heat, heat the oil. Add the garlic and cook, stirring occasionally, until the garlic just turns light tan, about 1 minute. Stir in the beans, fresh tomatoes, and green onions and cook, stirring occasionally, until the tomatoes give off their liquid, about 5 minutes. Stir in the wine and simmer to blend the flavors, about 5 minutes. Stir in the canned tomatoes and cook until heated through, about 2 minutes. Remove from the heat and stir in the chopped basil. Season to taste with salt and pepper. Keep warm. (The sauce can be made up to 1 hour ahead and stored at room temperature. Reheat gently before serving.)

Generously oil the cooking grate, but don't let the oil drip onto the fire. Lightly brush the fish on both sides with vegetable oil, and season on both sides with salt and pepper. Place the fish on the grill, cover, and grill until the undersides are seared with grill marks, about 2 minutes. Uncover, rotate the fish 90 degrees to create attractive cross-hatching, re-cover, and cook for 2 minutes more. Carefully turn the fish fillets over, re-cover, and grill for 2 minutes. Uncover, rotate the fish 90 degrees, re-cover, and continue grilling until the fish is barely opaque when flaked in the thickest part, about 2 minutes more.

Transfer the fillets to warmed dinner plates. Spoon an equal amount of the beans and tomatoes over each fillet. Drizzle each serving with olive oil, garnish with the basil leaves, and serve immediately.

BIG EASY BBQ SHRIMP

In New Orleans, barbecue shrimp is neither grilled nor smoked. Instead, it is cooked with lots of spices and butter. I've put my own spin on the dish with this creamy sauté. To give the rich sauce a deep seafood flavor, I simmer the shrimp shells to make a stock and then reduce the stock to a syrupy base, a step that takes little effort but delivers Big Time. [CHEF RICHARD SILVA]

Serves 6

2 pounds extra-large (16/20 count) shrimp in the shell

1 tablespoon Creole Seasoning (page 41)

SAUCE BASE

1 tablespoon canola oil

½ cup finely chopped yellow onion

2 tablespoons finely chopped garlic

1 cup Worcestershire sauce

2 tablespoons Creole Seasoning (page 41)

3 lemons, peel and pith cut away and flesh quartered

3 bay leaves

3 tablespoons canola oil

1 cup heavy (whipping) cream

2 tablespoons unsalted butter

1 tablespoon finely chopped fresh chives

Crusty bread for serving

Peel the shrimp, leaving only the tail segment intact, and reserve the shells. Devein the shrimp. In a bowl, toss the shrimp evenly with the Creole Seasoning to coat evenly. Cover and refrigerate until ready to cook.

To make the Sauce Base, in a large saucepan over medium-high heat, heat the oil until hot but not smoking. Add the onion and garlic and cook, stirring almost constantly, until the onion begins to soften, about 1 minute. Stir in the reserved shrimp shells, 2 cups water, the Worcestershire sauce, Creole Seasoning, lemons, and bay leaves and bring to a boil. Reduce the heat to medium-low and simmer, uncovered, for 30 minutes. Remove from the heat and let cool for 15 minutes.

Strain the stock through a fine-mesh sieve into a small saucepan. Bring to a boil over high heat and cook until reduced to ⅓ cup thick, dark brown syrup, about 15 minutes. (The sauce base can be made up to 1 hour ahead and stored at room temperature. If necessary, reheat until fluid before using.)

In a very large, deep skillet over high heat, heat 1½ tablespoons of the oil until very hot but not smoking. Add half of the shrimp and spread in an even layer. Cook, turning the shrimp occasionally, just until the edges begin to look opaque, about 2 minutes. Transfer to a platter. Repeat with the remaining 1½ tablespoons oil and shrimp. Combine the shrimp in the skillet. Stir in the sauce base and the cream, and cook, stirring often, until the cream comes to a simmer and the shrimp are opaque throughout, about 3 minutes. Using a slotted spoon, mound the shrimp in a warmed deep platter. Reduce the heat to very low and whisk the butter into the sauce until incorporated.

Spoon the sauce over the shrimp and sprinkle with the chives. Serve immediately. Pass the bread at the table for dipping into the sauce.

CHEF'S NOTE: *The size of shrimp is designated by the number of shrimp per pound. For example, 21/25 means there are 21 to 25 shrimp to a pound. Terms like* large *or* jumbo *vary from state to state, but the indication is still helpful. In general, how the shrimp will be cooked will determine the size you need. For this dish, in which the shrimp are seared and then simmered, you need to use very large shrimp so they don't overcook by the time the sauce is finished. A stir-fry, for example, can be made with smaller shrimp.*

OVEN-ROASTED COD WITH POTATOES AND TOMATOES

This recipe, which I learned from my mother, has been a tradition in my family as far back as I can remember.
It was always served on Christmas and often prepared, with love, on other significant days. It is a great dish that can be served anytime
during the year. Roasting allows the flavors of the fish and tomatoes to mingle and concentrate at the same time.
Serve with a green salad and crusty bread for a wonderfully tasty meal. [VINCENT ROSSETTI]

Serves 6

4 tablespoons extra-virgin olive oil, plus more for the pan

1½ pounds red-skinned potatoes, peeled and halved

2 cloves garlic, finely chopped

1 can (28 ounces) whole Italian-style tomatoes in juice, drained

1 cup low-sodium chicken broth

¼ cup nonpareil capers, drained

1 tablespoon chopped fresh basil

1 tablespoon chopped fresh oregano

½ cup coarsely chopped Kalamata olives

1 tablespoon chopped fresh flat-leaf parsley

2½ pounds skinless cod fillets

1 teaspoon kosher salt

1 teaspoon freshly ground black pepper

¼ cup freshly grated Parmesan cheese, preferably Parmigiano-Reggiano

Preheat the oven to 350°F. Lightly oil a deep roasting pan just large enough to hold the fillets in a single layer.

Place the potatoes in a saucepan and cover with lightly salted water. Bring to a boil over high heat and cook until the potatoes are barely tender when pierced with a fork, about 12 minutes. Drain the potatoes and set aside.

In a heavy-bottomed saucepan over medium heat, heat 1 tablespoon of the oil. Add the garlic and cook, stirring often, until it begins to turn tan, about 1 minute. Add the tomatoes and broth and bring to a boil, breaking up the tomatoes with the side of a spoon. Stir in the capers, basil, and oregano. Reduce the heat to medium-low and simmer for 5 minutes. Stir in the potatoes, return to a simmer, and cook until the tomato juices thicken, about 5 minutes. Remove from the heat and gently stir in the olives and parsley.

Pat the fish dry with paper towels. Season on both sides with the salt and pepper. Arrange the fillets in the prepared pan, cutting them as needed so they fit, and gently pour the potato mixture on top. The fish should be covered with the potato mixture; add additional broth or water, if needed.

Bake until the potatoes are completely tender and the fish is cooked through when tested with a fork, about 25 minutes.

Drizzle with the remaining 3 tablespoons oil and sprinkle with the Parmesan. Serve immediately.

TRADITIONAL CRAB CAKES WITH REMOULADE SAUCE

I can't believe that neither of our first two cookbooks, *Nordstrom Friends and Family* nor *Nordstrom Entertaining at Home*, contains this recipe for crab cakes, as it is one of the most popular dishes in our restaurants. Carefully follow the instructions (the rest period before forming the cakes is especially important), and you will make crab cakes for the most discerning palate. Remoulade is the classic accompaniment. [CHEF MICHAEL NORTHERN]

Serves 5

CRAB CAKES

1 cup mayonnaise

1 large egg

1½ teaspoons Old Bay seasoning

1½ teaspoons Sriracha chile sauce

1½ tablespoons finely chopped fresh chives

1½ tablespoons chopped fresh flat-leaf parsley

1 pound jumbo lump crabmeat, preferably pasteurized, drained and picked over for shell bits

1 cup *panko* (Japanese bread crumbs)

¼ teaspoon kosher salt

Pinch of freshly ground black pepper

REMOULADE SAUCE

1 cup mayonnaise

2 tablespoons minced sour gherkins

2 tablespoons minced red onion

1 tablespoon minced nonpareil capers

1 tablespoon chopped fresh flat-leaf parsley

2 teaspoons fresh lemon juice

¼ teaspoon Tabasco sauce

¼ teaspoon Old Bay seasoning

Pinch of freshly ground black pepper

4 tablespoons (½ stick) unsalted butter, melted

To make the Crab Cakes, in a large bowl, whisk together the mayonnaise, egg, Old Bay seasoning, chile sauce, chives, and parsley until well combined. Add the crabmeat and fold in gently with a rubber spatula. Sprinkle ½ cup of the *panko* over the mixture, and fold in gently, taking care not to break up the crabmeat. Cover with plastic wrap and refrigerate for 10 minutes. Remove from the refrigerator and fold in the remaining ½ cup *panko*. Season with the salt and pepper. Cover tightly with plastic wrap and refrigerate for at least 3 hours or up to 12 hours.

Meanwhile, make the Remoulade Sauce. In a small bowl, whisk together the mayonnaise, gherkins, onion, capers, parsley, lemon juice, Tabasco, Old Bay seasoning, and pepper until well combined. Cover and refrigerate until serving or for up to 3 days.

Divide the crabmeat mixture into 10 equal portions. Carefully form each portion into a barrel-shaped cake about 2½ inches in diameter and 1¼ inches tall.

Preheat the oven to 450°F. Choose a large ovenproof skillet to hold the crab cakes without crowding, and place in the oven for 7 minutes to preheat.

Remove the preheated skillet from the oven, and brush the bottom with about half of the butter. Arrange the crab cakes in the skillet, being careful they don't touch one another. Brush the tops of the cakes with the remaining butter.

Roast the crab cakes undisturbed until the undersides are golden brown, about 6 minutes. Remove from the oven and, using tongs and a thin metal spatula, gently flip over the crab cakes. Return the crab cakes to the oven and continue roasting until heated through and both sides are golden brown, about 3 minutes more.

Divide the crab cakes among warmed plates, placing 2 cakes on each plate, position a spoonful of the remoulade alongside. Serve immediately.

CHEF'S NOTE: *For consistent quality from city to city, we insist on pasteurized jumbo lump crab-meat, which consists of only "prime" nuggets from the body of the crustacean.*

CRAB-STUFFED MUSHROOMS

One of the true pleasures of being in the Pacific Northwest is the availability of fresh Dungeness crab.
Although this species is found from Alaska to Mexico, it is named for a little town in Washington where crab is king.
Any crabmeat will do, but aficionados like me will tell you that no crab is as sweet as Dungeness.
These appetizers can be made a few hours ahead and then baked just as
your guests arrive for a tasty welcome. [VINCENT ROSSETTI]

Serves 6

30 large cremini mushrooms

1½ tablespoons extra-virgin olive oil

¼ cup finely chopped yellow onion

2 cloves garlic, minced

4 ounces cream cheese, at room
temperature

1 teaspoon mayonnaise

¼ teaspoon Tabasco sauce

½ cup freshly grated Parmesan
cheese, preferably Parmigiano-
Reggiano

¾ pound crabmeat, preferably
Dungeness, picked over for
shell bits

Kosher salt

2 tablespoons finely chopped
fresh chives

Remove the stems from the mushrooms, and finely chop the stems. Set the caps and stems aside separately.

In a large skillet over medium-high heat, heat the oil. Add the chopped mushroom stems, onion, and garlic and cook, stirring often, until the mushroom stems give off their liquid and it evaporates, about 5 minutes. Let cool completely.

Preheat the oven to 375°F.

In a large bowl, mash together the cream cheese, mayonnaise, and Tabasco with a rubber spatula until well combined. Mix in the mushroom mixture and ¼ cup of the Parmesan. Fold in the crabmeat. Season with salt.

Fill each mushroom cap with some of the crab mixture, mounding it slightly. Sprinkle the filled mushrooms with the remaining ¼ cup Parmesan. Arrange the stuffed mushrooms on a rimmed baking sheet. (The mushrooms can be prepared to this point, covered with plastic wrap, and refrigerated for up to 8 hours before baking and serving.)

Bake the mushrooms until the mushrooms are tender, the filling is hot, and the cheese is golden brown, about 15 minutes. Let cool for 5 minutes. Transfer to a platter, sprinkle with the chives, and serve immediately.

PACIFIC RIM SEAFOOD CHOWDER

With its creamy base, potatoes, and seafood, this could technically be called a chowder, but it has its roots firmly in Asia, not New England. When I am looking for a light and satisfying one-dish meal to serve to company, I often make this soup that boasts flavor influences from all around the Pacific Rim. Adjust the seafood according to your preferences and what's available, such as substituting mussels for the clams or snapper for the halibut. [CHEF MICHAEL LYLE]

Serves 6

CHOWDER BASE

3 tablespoons canola oil

1 small yellow onion, finely chopped

1 tablespoon peeled and minced
    fresh ginger

3 bottles (8 ounces each) clam juice

2 cans (14 ounces each) unsweetened
    coconut milk, well shaken

½ cup low-sodium soy sauce

½ cup fresh lime juice

1 tablespoon plus 1 teaspoon
    Sriracha chile sauce

3 small Red Bliss potatoes, peeled,
    cut into ¼-inch dice

1 can (15 ounces) broken straw
    mushrooms, rinsed and drained

18 littleneck clams, scrubbed

½ pound skinless halibut fillet

½ pound large (21/25 count)
    shrimp, peeled and deveined

½ pound sea scallops, small tough
    side muscle removed, halved
    vertically

¼ pound cleaned calamari bodies,
    cut into ½-inch-wide rings

¼ cup cornstarch

3 tablespoons chopped fresh cilantro

1 tablespoon finely chopped fresh
    flat-leaf parsley

Kosher salt

Freshly ground black pepper

To make the Chowder Base, in a large soup pot over medium-low heat, heat the oil. Add the onion and cook, stirring often, until translucent, about 3 minutes. Stir in the ginger and cook until fragrant, about 30 seconds. Stir in the clam juice, coconut milk, soy sauce, lime juice, and chile sauce. Add the potatoes and mushrooms, raise the heat to medium-high, cover, and bring just to a simmer. Uncover, reduce the heat to medium-low, and simmer, stirring occasionally, to blend the flavors, about 30 minutes.

Discard any open clams that don't close when rapped. Cut the halibut fillet into 1-inch pieces. Stir in the clams, halibut, shrimp, and scallops, immersing them completely in the liquid. Cover, increase the heat to high, and return the soup to a simmer. Then return the heat to medium-low and simmer until all of the clams have opened, about 7 minutes. Discard any unopened clams. Stir in the calamari and cook, uncovered, just until heated through, about 1 minute.

In a small bowl, dissolve the cornstarch in ¼ cup water, and stir into the soup. Raise the heat to medium so the soup comes to a gentle boil and thickens. Remove from the heat and add the cilantro and parsley. Season to taste with salt and pepper.

Divide the soup evenly among warmed deep bowls. Serve hot.

SLOW COOKED

SUPER SAUCY BRAISED BRISKET

My Auntie Ethel and Uncle Marvin are famous in my family for their Lick-the-Plate-Clean Brisket. I was so inspired by my childhood memories of their dish that I created my own version, which is even richer and saucier. The extra sauce means you have plenty to pour over mashed potatoes or buttered noodles. Like most briskets, this one tastes even better when it cools in the sauce and is reheated and served the next day. [CHEF KIMBERLY HAZARD]

Serves 8 to 10

1 whole beef brisket (9 pounds), untrimmed

Kosher salt

Freshly ground black pepper

1 tablespoon granulated garlic

1 tablespoon dried thyme

4 tablespoons vegetable oil

4 yellow onions, thinly sliced

5 large carrots, peeled and grated on the large holes of a box grater

1 can (6 ounces) tomato paste

1 cup ketchup

½ cup firmly packed dark brown sugar

1 bottle (750 ml) hearty red wine, preferably Cabernet Sauvignon

4 cups low-sodium beef broth

1 bay leaf

CHEF'S NOTE: *You will need a very large Dutch oven or flameproof casserole to cook the brisket, even though the brisket shrinks dramatically during cooking. If you don't have a single Dutch oven large enough to hold both brisket halves, place each half in its own pot, and divide the cooking liquid between them.*

Cut the brisket in half crosswise. Rinse both halves with cold water and pat them dry. In a small bowl, mix together 3 tablespoons salt, 1 tablespoon pepper, the granulated garlic, and the thyme. Rub the mixture all over both brisket halves.

In a large skillet over medium-high heat, heat 2 tablespoons of the oil. Add 1 brisket half, fat side down. Cook until the underside is well browned, about 8 minutes. Turn the brisket over and brown the other side, about 8 minutes more. Transfer the brisket to a large platter. Repeat with the remaining 2 tablespoons oil and brisket half.

Position a rack in the lower third of the oven and preheat to 325°F.

Pour off all but 4 tablespoons of the fat from the skillet. Add the onions and carrots and cook, stirring often, until the onions are golden, about 15 minutes. Season with salt and pepper and stir well. Stir in the tomato paste and cook, stirring occasionally, until it darkens a shade, about 3 minutes. Stir in the ketchup and brown sugar until incorporated. Stir in the wine and bring to a boil, stirring to release any browned bits on the pan bottom. Cook, stirring occasionally, until the liquid begins to thicken, about 15 minutes. Add 2 cups of the broth and the bay leaf.

Stack the brisket halves in a very large Dutch oven or flameproof covered casserole. Pour in the wine mixture and bring to a boil over high heat. Cover the Dutch oven with aluminum foil, and then fit the lid on top.

Transfer the pot to the oven and cook the brisket for 2 hours. Remove from the oven and uncover. Transfer the brisket halves to a platter. Skim off and discard the fat from the cooking liquid. Pour the remaining 2 cups broth into the pot and bring the liquid to a simmer over high heat. Return the brisket halves to the pot. Replace the foil and lid, and continue cooking in the oven until the brisket is very tender when pierced with a meat fork, about 2 hours more. Uncover and let stand for 20 minutes. Remove the bay leaf and discard.

Transfer the brisket to a carving board. Skim off and discard the fat from the cooking liquid. Using a carving knife held on a slight diagonal, cut the brisket across the grain into ¼-inch-thick slices. Transfer the slices to a warmed deep platter. Spoon some of the sauce over the brisket, and pour the remaining sauce into a warmed large sauceboat. Serve the brisket hot, and pass the sauceboat at the table.

VIETNAMESE CARAMEL CHICKEN WITH CARROTS AND SNOW PEAS

This recipe may not seem like it belongs in this chapter because the last step goes quickly. But a long-simmered stock is critical to its success. The stock is simmered and reduced twice, and then further reinforced with a flavorful caramelization of garlic, ginger, sugar, soy sauce, and chile sauce to provide a subtle depth of flavors. [CHEF MICHAEL NORTHERN]

Serves 6

DOUBLE-RICH CHICKEN STOCK

5 pounds chicken backs and necks

1 yellow onion, roughly chopped

7 celery stalks, roughly chopped

3 large carrots, roughly chopped

2 bay leaves

2 teaspoons black peppercorns

25 fresh parsley stems
(reserve leaves for another use)

CARAMELIZED CHICKEN STOCK

½ cup granulated sugar

⅓ cup cloves garlic, thinly sliced

⅓ cup peeled and thinly sliced
fresh ginger

¼ cup soy sauce

1 tablespoon Chinese chile sauce
with garlic

5 cups Double-Rich Chicken Stock

Fine sea salt

ROASTED SHIITAKE MUSHROOMS

½ pound shiitake mushrooms, stems
removed and caps quartered

1 tablespoon Asian sesame oil

2 tablespoons canola oil

Fine sea salt

Freshly ground black pepper

To make the Double-Rich Chicken Stock, preheat the oven to 400°F. Divide the chicken, onion, celery, and carrots between 2 rimmed heavy-duty baking sheets.

Roast, stirring occasionally, until the chicken and vegetables are well browned, about 1 hour and 20 minutes. Let cool slightly, then transfer the chicken pieces and vegetables to a large stockpot. Discard the rendered fat in the baking sheets. While the baking sheets are still warm, pour 2 cups warm water into each pan and scrape up the browned bits on the pan bottoms with a wooden spatula. Carefully pour the liquid from the baking sheets into the stockpot and add cold water to cover the chicken and vegetables by 1 inch. Add the bay leaves, peppercorns, and parsley stems. Bring to a gentle boil over medium-high heat, reduce the temperature to low, and simmer gently, uncovered, occasionally skimming off any froth, until well flavored, about 4 hours.

Strain the stock through a colander over a large bowl. Strain the stock again, this time through a fine-mesh sieve set over another bowl. Let stand for 10 minutes. Skim off the clear yellow fat that rises to the surface. Rinse the pot, return the strained stock to it, and bring to a boil over medium heat. Boil until reduced by half (you should have about 5 cups), about 2 hours. Keep the stock hot.

To make the Caramelized Chicken Stock, in a heavy-bottomed nonstick saucepan, combine the sugar, garlic, and ginger. Cook over medium-low heat, stirring constantly, until the sugar is melted and caramelized to deep amber, about 15 minutes. Remove from heat and carefully stir in the soy sauce and chile sauce. The caramel will bubble and absorb the sauces. Stir in 1 cup of the hot reduced stock, mixing well to dissolve the caramel (return the pan to medium heat, if necessary, to dissolve it). Add the remaining 4 cups hot stock and bring to a simmer over high heat. Reduce the heat to medium-low and simmer to blend the flavors, about 15 minutes. Strain through a fine-mesh sieve set over a bowl. Season to taste with salt.

While the stock simmers, make the Roasted Shiitake Mushrooms. Preheat the oven to 400°F. In a small bowl, toss the mushrooms with the sesame and canola oils, then season with salt and pepper. Transfer the mushrooms to a rimmed baking sheet, spreading them in a single layer. Roast until the mushrooms are sizzling, about 5 minutes. Remove from the oven.

continued ›

1 pound skinless, boneless chicken breasts, trimmed of excess fat and cut into ¾-inch cubes

3 carrots, peeled and cut on the diagonal into ⅛-inch-thick slices

½ pound snow peas, stems and strings removed and halved on the diagonal

Hot steamed jasmine rice for serving

In a Dutch oven, combine the caramelized stock, cubed chicken, carrots, snow peas, and mushrooms over high heat. Cover tightly and cook until you see steam escaping from under the lid. Then continue to cook, covered, until the vegetables are crisp-tender and the chicken is cooked through, about 2 minutes.

Bring the Dutch oven to the table and open the lid so your guests can enjoy the aromas. Ladle into warmed bowls, and pass the rice at the table.

CHEF'S NOTE: *For an interesting, authentic presentation, serve the caramel chicken in individual Asian clay pots, preferably the type netted in wire, available at Asian markets. For the first few uses, until the pots are well broken in, soak the tops and bottoms in warm water to cover for 1 hour, then drain. Divide the chicken, vegetables, and stock evenly among 6 soaked and drained pots, cover, and heat each over medium–high heat until a steady plume of steam emits through the lid's steam vent. Cook for 2 minutes. (If you have only 4 burners, cook 3 pots at a time, as the first group will stay hot while you are heating the second batch.) Using pot holders, set each pot on a heatproof plate, to act as a liner, and serve.*

OXTAIL STEW

If you want to make the best beef stew, oxtails are your answer, even though diners have to deal with lots of bones. As the oxtails cook, these tough nuggets release plenty of collagen and gelatin into the cooking liquid, giving the sauce an unbelievable consistency and flavor that you won't get from boneless cuts. You will have a difficult time deciding which is better: the meat, the vegetables, or the beautifully spiced broth. Don't forget the crusty bread to sop up every last drop. [CHEF JONATHAN ROHLAND]

Serves 6

SPICE BOUQUET

2 teaspoons black peppercorns

4 fresh thyme sprigs

2 fresh rosemary sprigs

2 fresh flat-leaf parsley sprigs

2 bay leaves

3 pounds oxtails, cut 2 inches thick

Kosher salt

Freshly ground black pepper

¼ cup extra-virgin olive oil

2 tablespoons unsalted butter

½ pound white boiling onions, peeled (see Chef's Note)

3 celery stalks, cut into ½-inch dice

6 cloves garlic, coarsely chopped

2 tablespoons tomato paste

1 cup dry red wine such as Cabernet Sauvignon

8 cups low-sodium beef broth

1 can (14½ ounces) diced tomatoes in juice

2 carrots, peeled and cut into ½-inch dice

2 small parsnips, peeled and cut into ½-inch dice

To make the Spice Bouquet, rinse a 9-inch square of cheesecloth with water and squeeze out the excess water. Place the peppercorns, thyme, rosemary, parsley, and bay leaves on the cheesecloth, bring the corners together, and tie into a packet with kitchen string.

Rinse the oxtails under cold water and pat dry with paper towels. Season the oxtails with 2 teaspoons salt and 1 teaspoon pepper.

In a large Dutch oven over medium-high heat, heat the oil until very hot but not smoking. Working in batches to avoid crowding, add the oxtails and cook, turning occasionally, until browned and crisp on all sides, about 10 minutes. Using a slotted spoon, transfer to paper towels to drain.

Drain off the fat from the pot, but don't discard the browned bits. Return the pot to medium-high heat and add the butter. Add the onions, celery, and garlic and cook, stirring occasionally and scraping up the browned bits on the pot bottom with a wooden spatula, until the onions begin to brown, about 5 minutes. Stir in the tomato paste and cook for 1 minute more. Stir in the wine, bring to a boil, and cook until it has nearly evaporated, about 5 minutes. Add the broth, tomatoes and their juice, 1½ cups water, and the spice bouquet. Return the oxtails to the pot and return the liquid to a boil.

Cover tightly, reduce the heat to medium-low, and simmer, stirring occasionally, for 1½ hours. Uncover and simmer, skimming off any fat that rises to the surface, for 45 minutes. Stir in the carrots and parsnips and add more water, if needed, to cover them. Continue cooking and skimming off the fat until the oxtails are very tender, about 45 minutes more. The total cooking time is about 3 hours.

Remove and discard the spice bouquet. Season the stew with salt and pepper. Ladle into warmed shallow bowls and serve hot.

CHEF'S NOTE: *To peel boiling onions, bring a pot of water to a boil over high heat. Add the onions and cook until the skins loosen, about 1 minute. Drain and rinse under cold running water. Trim off the top and bottom from each onion. To help the onions keep their shape (not telescope) during cooking, score the cut areas with an X. Make a slit down one side, and peel away the skin.*

JAROD'S CRISP FRENCH BAGUETTES

This is a fairly easy recipe that produces superior results. To prove my point, my young son, Jarod, has become the bread baker in our family. Chilling the dough overnight allows it to develop a yeasty flavor and delicate crumb. To replicate the steam in a professional oven, which gives the browned crust a glossy sheen, use a spray bottle. [CHEF MICHAEL NORTHERN]
Makes 3 baguettes

5 cups (1½ pounds) unbleached all-purpose flour, plus more for kneading

1 tablespoon kosher salt

2 cups warm (105° to 115°F) water

2 packages (2¼ teaspoons each) active dry yeast

The day before baking the bread, in a large bowl, whisk together the 5 cups flour and salt to mix well. Pour the warm water into another large bowl, sprinkle in the yeast, and let stand until foamy, about 5 minutes. Whisk to dissolve the yeast.

Whisk the flour mixture, 1 cup at a time, into the yeast mixture, whisking after each addition until the batter is smooth before adding more. When the batter becomes too thick to whisk, change over to a wooden spoon. Add enough of the flour mixture to make a stiff, but moist dough.

Turn the dough out onto a floured work surface. Knead the dough forcefully by hand, adding more flour (up to ¾ cup) as needed to keep the dough from sticking to the surface, until the dough is smooth and elastic, about 8 minutes. Every now and then, pick up the dough and smack it firmly down onto the surface—it's good for the dough!

Form the dough into a ball and place it in a very large bowl that will accommodate its rise to triple in size. Cover the bowl with a damp kitchen towel and let stand at room temperature in a draft-free place until the dough has doubled in volume, about 4 hours, depending on the temperature of the kitchen. (The temperature should not be too high here; let the dough rise slowly at this point in a relatively cool, not warm, place.)

Punch down the dough. Cover the bowl tightly with plastic wrap. Refrigerate for at least 12 hours or up to 18 hours.

Remove the dough from the refrigerator and let stand at room temperature until it loses its chill and begins to rise, 3 to 4 hours. Punch down the dough. Cut into 3 equal portions (if you use a kitchen scale, they will weigh about 13 ounces each) and shape each portion into a ball. Put the balls on the work surface and cover with a damp kitchen towel.

On a clean work surface, press 1 ball of dough into a 7-inch square. Starting at the top of the square, roll the dough toward you, forming a tight cylinder about 1½ inches in diameter. Place the cylinder under the towel to relax for 5 minutes. Repeat with the other 2 dough balls.

continued >

Line a heavy-gauge 18-by-13-inch baking sheet (also called a half sheet pan) with parchment paper and dust the paper with flour. Return the first cylinder you formed to the work surface. Using your fingertips, roll the cylinder back and forth, applying moderate pressure while gradually and evenly lengthening the dough into a loaf about 14 inches long. Place on the baking sheet. Repeat with the remaining 2 dough cylinders, spacing the 3 loaves at least 1½ inches apart on the baking sheet. Cover the loaves with dampened lightweight, lint-free kitchen towels. Let stand in a warm, draft-free place (such as near a turned-on stove) until doubled in size, about 1½ hours.

At least 30 minutes before baking the bread, preheat the oven to 475°F.

Using a straight-edged razor or a very sharp, thin-bladed knife, slash each loaf with 4 or 5 shallow, diagonal cuts. Fill a spray bottle with water, set the nozzle on fine mist, and evenly spray the tops and sides of the loaves.

Put the sheet with the loaves into the oven and immediately reduce the temperature to 425°F. Bake for 3 minutes, and then very quickly mist the loaves with water. Continue baking, spraying the loaves every 5 minutes and rotating the pan 180 degrees halfway through baking, until the loaves are evenly yet lightly browned and sound hollow when tapped on the bottoms, about 20 minutes. Let cool on wire racks until warm or to room temperature.

CHEF'S NOTE: *Resist the temptation to use a stand mixer to prepare this recipe. One of the reasons the loaves come out so well is because nothing can replace kneading by hand. Somehow the dough knows the difference.*

BRAISED CHICKEN WITH BALSAMIC VINEGAR AND PORCINI MUSHROOMS

This is not your average chicken in a pot, but a symphony of flavors: tart vinegar, smoky bacon, and earthy mushrooms. You'll have a good amount of the delicious sauce to pour over fettuccine or mashed potatoes. [CHEF CORY GOODMAN]

Serves 4

2 ounces dried porcini mushrooms
 (2 loosely packed cups)

2 cups boiling water

2 tablespoons extra-virgin olive oil

½ pound thick-sliced bacon,
 preferably apple wood smoked,
 cut crosswise into ¼-inch pieces

¾ cup all-purpose flour

Kosher salt

Freshly ground black pepper

1 whole chicken (3½ pounds),
 cut into 8 serving pieces

 1 yellow onion, chopped

4 cloves garlic, chopped

¼ cup balsamic vinegar

1 can (14½ ounces) diced tomatoes
 in juice, drained with ¼ cup juice
 reserved

1 cup low-sodium chicken broth

½ cup dry white wine

1 teaspoon chopped fresh thyme

½ teaspoon chopped fresh rosemary

In a heatproof bowl, combine the mushrooms and boiling water. Let stand until the mushrooms soften, about 20 minutes. Lift the mushrooms out of the water and set aside. Carefully strain the soaking liquid through a fine-mesh sieve into a small saucepan, leaving the grit behind in the bottom of the bowl. Bring to a boil over high heat and boil until reduced to ½ cup. Set aside.

Meanwhile, in a large skillet or Dutch oven over medium heat, heat the oil. Add the bacon and cook, stirring occasionally, until the bacon is crisp around the edges, about 5 minutes. Remove the pan from the heat. Using a slotted spoon, transfer the bacon to paper towels to drain.

In a shallow dish, stir together the flour, 2 teaspoons salt, and 1 teaspoon pepper. Coat the chicken pieces, one at a time, in the seasoned flour, shaking off the excess. Return the skillet to medium heat. Working in batches to avoid crowding, add the chicken, skin side down, to the skillet and cook, turning once or twice, until golden brown on both sides, about 10 minutes. Transfer to a platter.

Pour off all but 2 tablespoons of the fat from the skillet and return to medium-high heat. Add the onion and cook, stirring often, until translucent, about 5 minutes. Stir in the garlic and cook, stirring often, until the onion is golden (be careful not to burn the garlic), about 5 minutes more. Add the vinegar and boil until almost evaporated. Stir in the tomatoes and ¼ cup juice, broth, wine, and reduced porcini liquid and bring to a boil.

Return the chicken to the pan. Bring back to a boil, then reduce the heat to medium-low, cover, and simmer for 10 minutes. Add the bacon, thyme, rosemary, and reserved mushrooms. Turn the chicken, re-cover, and continue cooking until the chicken shows no sign of pink when pierced at the bone, about 15 minutes more. Season to taste with salt and pepper.

Transfer the chicken and sauce to a warmed deep platter and serve immediately.

CHICKEN RISOTTO WITH SHIITAKE MUSHROOMS, ROSEMARY, AND ROASTED GARLIC

Garlic and rosemary are often matched with chicken, and for good reason.
Instead of the usual roasted or grilled preparations, here is the trio in risotto. [CHEF RICHARD VENZOR]

Serves 4

2 skinless, boneless chicken breast halves (about 6 ounces each), trimmed of excess fat

Kosher salt

Freshly ground black pepper

2 teaspoons chopped fresh rosemary

3 tablespoons extra-virgin olive oil

1 can (49 ounces) low-sodium chicken broth

4 tablespoons (½ stick) unsalted butter

6 ounces shiitake mushrooms, stems removed and caps cut into narrow strips

1 yellow onion, finely chopped

2 cups medium-grain Italian rice such as Arborio, Vialone Nano, or Carnaroli

½ cup dry white wine

6 ounces grape tomatoes, cored and halved lengthwise

½ cup freshly grated Parmesan cheese, preferably Parmigiano-Reggiano, plus a wedge for garnish

½ cup whole Simple Roasted Garlic cloves (page 61), halved lengthwise

Preheat the oven to 300°F. Line a rimmed baking sheet with parchment paper.

Season the chicken on both sides with 1 teaspoon salt and ½ teaspoon pepper. Sprinkle the chicken on both sides with the rosemary, patting it to help it adhere.

In a large skillet over medium-high heat, heat the oil until very hot but not smoking. Add the chicken and cook until the undersides are beginning to brown, about 1 minute. Turn the chicken and lightly brown the second sides, about 1 minute more. Transfer the chicken to the baking sheet and roast until the juices run clear when the flesh is pierced with the tip of a sharp knife, about 15 minutes. Transfer to a carving board and let cool completely. Using your fingers, pull the chicken into fine strands. Set aside.

In a saucepan, bring the broth just to a simmer over medium heat. Reduce the heat to very low to keep the broth hot.

In a deep, wide saucepan or Dutch oven over medium heat, melt 3 tablespoons of the butter. Add the mushrooms and cook, stirring occasionally, until beginning to brown, about 3 minutes. Add the onion and cook, stirring occasionally, until translucent, about 3 minutes more. Add the rice and stir until the kernels are covered with the butter and the rice feels heavy in the spoon (do not toast the rice), about 2 minutes. Add the wine and cook, stirring constantly, until the wine has almost evaporated.

Add ½ cup of the hot broth to the rice and cook, stirring frequently, until the rice has almost completely absorbed the liquid. Adjust the heat to medium-low to keep the risotto at a steady slow simmer. Continue adding the broth, ½ cup at a time, stirring until the broth is almost completely absorbed before adding the next addition and leaving ¼ cup broth for the final addition. After about 18 minutes, the rice grains will be creamy, plump, and cooked through but still slightly chewy. If you run out of broth before the risotto reaches this point, use hot water. Stir in the remaining ¼ cup broth and the tomatoes and cook for about 30 seconds to warm the tomatoes. Fold in the remaining 1 tablespoon butter along with the Parmesan, rosemary-coated chicken, and roasted garlic. Season to taste with salt and pepper.

Spoon the risotto into warmed shallow bowls. Using a vegetable peeler, shave curls of Parmesan over each serving. Serve immediately.

SLOW-BRAISED SHORT RIBS

*In the chef's bag of tricks, braised short ribs are a surefire hit. They are meatier than pork or lamb ribs,
and have a delicious melting quality that can't be beat. Use the leftover beef to make Crispy Short Ribs (page 97),
or brush the ribs with your favorite barbecue sauce and grill them up.* [CHEF MICHAEL LYLE]

Serves 6

BOUQUET GARNI

4 fresh rosemary sprigs

4 fresh thyme sprigs

1 teaspoon black peppercorns

3 bay leaves

**5 pounds bone-in beef short ribs,
about 1 inch thick, trimmed of
excess fat**

Kosher salt

Freshly ground black pepper

¼ cup extra-virgin olive oil

1 yellow onion, chopped

4 cloves garlic, minced

1½ cups dry red wine

4 cups low-sodium beef broth

1 can (8 ounces) tomato sauce

3 carrots, peeled and diced

2 celery stalks, chopped

Preheat the oven to 300° F.

To make the Bouquet Garni, rinse a 9-inch square of cheesecloth with water, and squeeze out the excess water. Place the rosemary, thyme, peppercorns, and bay leaves on the cheesecloth, bring the corners together, and tie into a packet with kitchen string.

To prepare the short ribs, season the ribs all over with 2 tablespoons salt and 1 tablespoon pepper. In a large Dutch oven over medium-high heat, heat the oil until very hot but not smoking. Working in batches to avoid crowding, add the short ribs and cook, turning occasionally, until browned on all sides, about 5 minutes. Transfer the short ribs to a platter.

Pour off all but 2 tablespoons of the fat from the pot and return the pot to medium-low heat. Add the onion and garlic and cook, stirring occasionally, until the onion turns golden brown, about 5 minutes. Add the wine and bring to a boil, stirring up the browned bits on the pot bottom with a wooden spatula. Boil until reduced to ½ cup, about 6 minutes. Stir in the broth, tomato sauce, and bouquet garni. Return the short ribs to the pot and add the carrots and celery. Cover the Dutch oven with aluminum foil, and then fit the lid on top.

Transfer the pot to the oven and cook until the short ribs are very tender when pierced with a meat fork, about 3 hours. Transfer the short ribs to a warmed deep platter and cover with foil to keep warm. Discard the bouquet garni.

Skim the fat from the surface of the cooking liquid. Using a slotted spoon, scoop up half of the vegetables and place in a blender. With the lid vented, and the machine running, gradually add 2 cups of the cooking liquid and process until smooth. Transfer to a small saucepan. Repeat with the remaining vegetables and 2 cups of the cooking liquid. Season the sauce to taste with salt and pepper and reheat gently over low heat.

Spoon the sauce over the short ribs. Serve immediately.

SPLIT PEA SOUP WITH CILANTRO

This soup is a twist on an old favorite, created through a group effort by two very talented cooks, Artemio Gonzalez and Miguel Ruiz. These two gentlemen, both from Cuba, felt that the American split pea soup lacked character. After much trial and error, we found the flavors we were looking for. The good old split pea is still there, but it has much more personality. This soup has become the most requested one in our repertoire. [CHEF KEITH BREEDLOVE]

Serves 8 to 10

1 pound (2½ cups) dried split peas

2 tablespoons extra-virgin olive oil

1 small carrot, peeled and cut into ¼-inch dice

½ small yellow onion, finely diced

1 celery stalk, cut into ¼-inch dice

½ small red bell pepper, seeded, deribbed, and cut into ¼-inch dice

1 tablespoon seeded and finely chopped jalapeño chile

1 teaspoon ground coriander

1 teaspoon dry mustard

Kosher salt

Freshly ground black pepper

1 can (49 ounces) low-sodium chicken broth

1 large Idaho or other baking potato, peeled and cut into ¼-inch dice

1 bay leaf

¼ cup whole milk

1 teaspoon soy sauce

¼ cup chopped fresh cilantro

2 tablespoons red wine vinegar

3 green onions, white and light green parts only, cut on the diagonal ⅛ inch thick

In a large saucepan over medium heat, combine the peas and 5 cups water and bring to a boil, taking care the peas do not boil over. Reduce the heat to medium-low, cover, and simmer, stirring occasionally, until most of the liquid is absorbed, about 20 minutes. Remove from the heat and let stand for 1 hour.

In a soup pot over medium-high heat, heat the oil. Add the carrot, onion, celery, bell pepper, and jalapeño and cook, stirring constantly, until the vegetables soften, about 4 minutes. Add the coriander, mustard, 1½ teaspoons salt, and ¾ teaspoon pepper, stir well, and cook for 2 minutes. Stir in the broth and bring to a boil, stirring constantly. Stir in the peas and their water and return to a boil. Add the potato and bay leaf and simmer, uncovered, until the potato and peas are tender, about 1 hour.

Remove the bay leaf and discard. Add the milk, soy sauce, and cilantro and heat until hot. Stir in the vinegar and season to taste with salt and pepper. If the soup seems too thick, thin with a little water. Ladle into warmed bowls and garnish with the green onions. Serve immediately.

LEMON RISOTTO WITH GRILLED SHRIMP AND ASPARAGUS

A little lemon juice goes a long way toward brightening flavors.
Think of the ubiquitous lemon wedge served with seafood as proof. In this creamy risotto,
the citrus acts as a foil to both the shrimp and the asparagus. [CHEF TONY COLABELLI]

Serves 4

1 pound extra-large (16/20 count) shrimp in the shell (see Chef's Note, page 142)

2 tablespoons extra-virgin olive oil

Kosher salt

Freshly ground black pepper

¾ pound thin asparagus, woody stem ends removed, cut into 4-inch lengths

1 can (49 ounces) low-sodium chicken broth

4 tablespoons (½ stick) unsalted butter

½ white onion, finely chopped

2 cups Italian medium-grain rice such as Arborio, Vialone Nano, or Carnaroli

½ cup dry white wine

¼ cup fresh lemon juice

½ cup freshly grated Parmesan cheese, preferably Parmigiano-Reggiano, plus more for serving

Prepare a medium-hot fire in a charcoal grill, or preheat a gas grill on medium (see Chef's Note, page 126). Preheat the oven to 300°F.

One at a time, peel the shrimp, then cut down the center along the back to the tail, cutting almost all of the way through. Open the shrimp until it lies flat and lift out the vein with the tip of the knife or your fingers.

In a bowl, toss the shrimp with 1 tablespoon of the oil and ½ teaspoon salt. In another bowl, toss the asparagus with the remaining 1 tablespoon oil, ½ teaspoon salt, and ¼ teaspoon pepper. Place the shrimp on the grill and cook, turning occasionally, until they are opaque, about 3 minutes. Transfer to an ovenproof platter.

Place the asparagus spears on the grill, arranging them perpendicular to the grid so they don't fall through. Grill the asparagus, turning as needed, until seared with grill marks and crisp-tender, about 5 minutes. Transfer to the platter with the shrimp. Cover with plastic wrap and set aside.

In a saucepan, bring the broth just to a simmer over medium heat. Reduce the heat to very low to keep the broth hot.

In a deep, wide saucepan or Dutch oven over medium heat, melt 3 tablespoons of the butter. Add the onion and cook, stirring occasionally, until translucent, about 3 minutes. Add the rice and stir until the kernels are covered with butter and the rice feels heavy in the spoon (do not toast the rice), about 2 minutes. Add the wine and cook, stirring constantly, until the wine has almost evaporated.

continued >

Add ½ cup of the hot broth to the rice and cook, stirring frequently, until the rice has almost completely absorbed the liquid. Adjust the heat to medium-low to keep the risotto at a steady slow simmer. Continue adding the broth, ½ cup at a time, stirring until the broth is almost completely absorbed before adding the next addition and leaving ¼ cup broth for the final addition. After about 18 minutes, the rice grains will be creamy, plump, and cooked through but still slightly chewy. If you run out of broth before the risotto reaches this point, use hot water. About 3 minutes before the risotto is done, uncover the shrimp and asparagus and place in the oven to heat through. Stir the remaining ¼ cup broth and the lemon juice into the rice, and then fold in the remaining 1 tablespoon butter along with the Parmesan. Season to taste with salt and pepper.

Spoon the risotto into warmed shallow bowls. Scatter the asparagus over the top, dividing it evenly. Using tongs, embed 4 grilled shrimp, tails pointing up, around the perimeter of each serving. Serve hot, and pass Parmesan cheese at the table.

CHEF'S NOTE: *To ensure risotto has the proper creamy texture, you must use medium-grain rice with a high starch content, and stir the rice constantly to help release the starch into the cooking liquid. While Arborio rice is the most common Italian medium-grain rice, look for other varieties, such as Vialone Nano and Carnaroli. There is nothing wrong with Arborio, but the latter are even starchier, and make especially unctuous and refined risottos.*

.

BRAISED CHICKEN LEGS WITH ROASTED GARLIC JUS

Chicken breasts are so popular that it is easy to overlook economical, tasty chicken legs. They take well to braising, where they can exchange flavors with the cooking liquid. This stew is redolent with red wine and roast garlic, and should be served over creamy polenta or some mashed potatoes. [CHEF RICHARD SILVA]

Serves 6

½ cup all-purpose flour

Kosher salt

Freshly ground black pepper

6 whole chicken legs

¼ cup extra-virgin olive oil, plus
 more for the pan

1 yellow onion, chopped

2 carrots, peeled and chopped

2 celery stalks, chopped

½ cup dry red wine

6 cups Double-Rich Chicken Stock
 (page 155), or 1 can (49 ounces)
 low-sodium chicken broth

2 bay leaves

6 tablespoons (¾ stick) unsalted
 butter

½ cup whole Simple Roasted Garlic
 cloves (page 61)

Preheat the oven to 325°F.

In a shallow dish, stir together the flour, 1 tablespoon salt, and 1 teaspoon pepper. One at a time, coat the chicken legs with the seasoned flour mixture, shaking off the excess. In a Dutch oven over medium-high heat, heat the oil until hot but not smoking. Working in batches to avoid crowding, add the chicken and cook, turning occasionally, until golden brown on all sides, about 7 minutes. Transfer to a plate.

Pour off all but 3 tablespoons of the oil from the pot and return it to medium heat. Add the onion, carrots, and celery and cook, stirring occasionally, until the vegetables soften, about 5 minutes. Pour in the wine and bring to a boil, scraping up the browned bits on the pot bottom with a wooden spatula. Return the chicken to the pot and cook until the wine is almost completely evaporated, about 5 minutes. Pour in the stock, add the bay leaves, and bring to a boil. Cover the pot, transfer it to the oven, and cook until the chicken is just tender, about 1¼ hours.

Meanwhile, oil a large rimmed baking sheet. When the chicken is ready, remove from the oven and, using a large slotted spoon, transfer the chicken legs to the prepared baking sheet. Increase the oven temperature to 400°F. Melt 2 tablespoons of the butter. Brush the chicken with the melted butter and season with salt and pepper. Roast until the skin is browned, about 15 minutes.

Meanwhile, strain the cooking liquid through a fine-mesh sieve set over a bowl; discard the solids in the sieve. Let the cooking liquid stand for a few minutes. Skim off the clear yellow fat that rises to the surface. Return the braising liquid to the Dutch oven and boil over high heat until reduced to about 1½ cups, about 15 minutes. Stir in the roasted garlic cloves and remove from the heat. Cut the remaining 4 tablespoons butter into small cubes. Whisk them, a few cubes at a time, into the sauce to thicken it lightly. Season to taste with salt and pepper.

To serve, place a leg in each of 6 warmed shallow bowls. Divide the sauce evenly among the bowls and serve hot.

FRUITS AND BERRIES

WHITE CHOCOLATE AND RASPBERRY BRUNCH PANCAKES

If you've ever had White Chocolate Bread Pudding, one of the most popular desserts at Nordstrom's Cafe Bistro restaurants, you'll be familiar with the flavor combination celebrated in these decadent pancakes. [CHEF MICHAEL NORTHERN]

Serves 4

1½ cups all-purpose flour

3 tablespoons sugar

2 teaspoons baking powder

¼ teaspoon fine sea salt

1 cup whole milk

2 large eggs, lightly beaten

3 tablespoons unsalted butter, melted and cooled, plus more for the griddle

1 pint raspberries

1 cup (6 ounces) white chocolate morsels

Powdered sugar for dusting

Preheat the oven to 200°F. Line a rimmed baking sheet with a clean kitchen towel, and have a few more towels ready.

In a large bowl, sift together the flour, sugar, baking powder, and salt. Make a well in the center. In another bowl, whisk together the milk, eggs, and butter, and pour the mixture into the well. Stir just until blended but still slightly lumpy. If the batter seems too thick, thin with a little water.

Heat a griddle or large, heavy nonstick skillet over medium-low heat until very hot. A few drops of cold water splashed on the bottom should dance across the surface. Lightly grease the griddle with butter. Using ⅓ cup batter for each pancake, pour the batter onto the griddle, creating pancakes about 4 inches in diameter and being careful not to crowd the griddle. Cook until bubbles just begin to appear on the surface, about 1½ minutes. Scatter about 4 raspberries and 7 white chocolate morsels over the top of each pancake. Cook until the pancakes are golden brown on the undersides, about 1 minute more. Turn the pancakes over and cook until the second sides are lightly browned, about 1 minute more. Transfer the pancakes to the baking sheet, cover with a towel, and keep warm in the oven. Repeat with the remaining batter, raspberries, and chocolate morsels, separating the layers of pancakes with the towels.

Arrange the pancakes on warmed plates, and scatter the remaining raspberries and chocolate morsels on top. Using a fine-mesh sieve, dust with powdered sugar, and then serve immediately.

CHEF'S NOTE: *Pancakes are always best when served the moment they are out of the pan. If your gathering is small, you may be able to cook them to order.*

BALSAMIC STRAWBERRY SHORTCAKE

Over the last few years, American cooks have discovered what Italians have known for years: balsamic vinegar goes great with strawberries. Here, old-fashioned strawberry shortcake is given a dramatic twist with a sweet-tart glaze made with balsamic vinegar and sugar. The recipe also illustrates the umami talents of balsamic vinegar as a flavor enhancer. [CHEF MICHAEL NORTHERN]

Serves 8

SHORTCAKES

⅔ cup (1¼ sticks) ice-cold unsalted butter, cut into ½-inch cubes, plus more for the pan

3½ cups all-purpose flour, plus more for the pan

⅓ cup granulated sugar, plus more for sprinkling

2 tablespoons baking powder

½ teaspoon fine sea salt

2 large eggs

½ cup heavy (whipping) cream, plus more for brushing the shortcakes

½ cup buttermilk

SWEETENED WHIPPED CREAM

3 cups heavy (whipping) cream

½ cup powdered sugar

1 teaspoon pure vanilla extract

STRAWBERRY TOPPING

2 pints strawberries, hulled and sliced lengthwise

1½ tablespoons granulated sugar

BALSAMIC DRIZZLE

½ cup balsamic vinegar

¼ cup granulated sugar

Powdered sugar for dusting

To make the Shortcakes, preheat the oven to 350°F. Butter a rimmed baking sheet. Dust the pan with flour and tap out the excess.

In the bowl of a stand mixer, sift together the flour, granulated sugar, baking powder, and salt. Scatter the butter over the flour mixture. Affix the bowl to the mixer, and fit the mixer with the paddle attachment. On medium speed, beat until the mixture is crumbly, about 2½ minutes. Beat in the eggs, one at a time, mixing well after each addition. The mixture will come together in a ball. In a small bowl, mix together the cream and buttermilk. On low speed, gradually beat in the cream mixture until a stiff, moist dough forms.

Using ½ cup of the dough for each shortcake (a 4-ounce spring-action ice cream scoop works well, or use a dry-measuring cup), portion the dough onto the prepared baking sheet, spacing the portions 1 inch apart, to make 8 shortcakes total. Brush the tops with cream, and sprinkle lightly with granulated sugar.

Bake the shortcakes until lightly browned, 20 to 25 minutes. Let cool on the baking sheet on a wire rack for 5 minutes. Transfer the shortcakes to the rack and let cool completely.

To make the Sweetened Whipped Cream, in a chilled large bowl, using the stand mixer fitted with the whisk attachment or a handheld mixer, whip the cream on medium-high speed until soft peaks form. Add the powdered sugar and vanilla and whip until the cream holds firm peaks. Cover and refrigerate until ready to use.

To make the Strawberry Topping, in a bowl, combine the strawberries and granulated sugar and toss gently to coat evenly. Let stand until the berries release some juices, about 30 minutes.

To make the Balsamic Drizzle, in a small saucepan over medium heat, combine the vinegar and granulated sugar and bring to a simmer. Cook until the mixture has reduced by nearly half and the glaze is syrupy, about 8 minutes. Set aside to cool slightly. (If the glaze thickens too much, dilute it with warm water until it is the consistency of chocolate syrup.)

For each serving, split a shortcake in half horizontally and place the bottom, cut side up, on a dessert plate. Top with some strawberries and then with some whipped cream. Using a spoon, streak the berries and cream with a drizzle of the balsamic glaze. Cap with the top half of the shortcake. Using a fine-mesh sieve, dust with powdered sugar and serve immediately.

ITALIAN MASCARPONE AND BERRY TRIFLE

Trifle is a rustic layered dessert beloved in both Britain and Italy (in the latter, it is known as *zuppa inglese*, or "English soup"). It is often made with a vanilla sauce and fruit preserves, but this version gets its creaminess from rich mascarpone cheese and its fresh tang from mixed berries. Present the trifle in its bowl at the table, and let everyone serve themselves with a big spoon. [CHEF MICHAEL LYLE]

Serves 6

SYRUP

½ cup orange-flavored liqueur such as Grand Marnier

½ cup granulated sugar

MASCARPONE CREAM

2 cups heavy (whipping) cream

¼ cup powdered sugar

1 container (8 ounces) mascarpone cheese, at room temperature

1 pound strawberries, hulled and sliced

1 pint raspberries

1 pint blueberries

1 pint blackberries

2 tablespoons granulated sugar

1 store-bought all-butter loaf cake (¾ pound), cut into ⅓-inch-thick slices

1 large fresh mint sprig

To make the Syrup, in a small saucepan over low heat, combine the liqueur, granulated sugar, and ½ cup water and bring to a simmer, stirring to dissolve the sugar. Remove from the heat and let cool completely.

To make the Mascarpone Cream, in a chilled bowl, using an electric mixer on medium speed, whip together the cream and powdered sugar until stiff peaks form. On low speed, add the mascarpone and mix just until blended.

To assemble the trifle, in a large bowl, combine the strawberries, raspberries, blueberries, and blackberries. Sprinkle with the granulated sugar and toss gently to mix evenly. Measure 1 cup of the berries and set aside for garnishing the trifle.

Arrange a layer of the cake slices in the bottom of a 4-quart clear-glass bowl, trimming the slices as needed to cover the bottom completely. Using a pastry brush, generously brush the cake with about one-third of the syrup. Spread with one-third of the mascarpone cream, and then top with half of the berries. Top the berries with another layer of cake, and brush the cake with half of the remaining syrup. Top the cake with half of the remaining mascarpone cream, and then the remaining berries. Finish with a final layer of cake, brush with the remaining syrup, and top with the remaining mascarpone cream. Garnish with the reserved 1 cup berries. Cover loosely with plastic wrap and refrigerate until chilled, at least 2 hours or up to 1 day.

Garnish with the mint sprig and serve chilled, spooned into bowls.

CHEF'S NOTE: *Mascarpone cheese is a buttery, spreadable cheese, available in both imported Italian and domestic versions. It is a staple ingredient in tiramisu and has many other uses. For a special breakfast, sweeten it with a little brown sugar and serve it on top of French toast. For a quick bruschetta, mix it with softened Gorgonzola cheese and spread on toasted slices of crusty country bread.*

LEMON RICOTTA HOTCAKES WITH BLUEBERRIES

This is a perfect dish to serve when gathering with friends for Sunday brunch or surprising
a loved one with breakfast in bed. The sweetness of the berries and acidity of the lemon provide an ideal flavor balance.
Cottage cheese can be substituted for the ricotta cheese. [CHEF JOE NOONAN]

Serves 4

¾ cup whole-milk ricotta cheese

3 large eggs, separated, at room temperature

4 tablespoons (½ stick) unsalted butter, melted and cooled

Grated zest of 2 lemons, plus more for garnish

¼ cup all-purpose flour

2 tablespoons granulated sugar

¼ teaspoon fine sea salt

Vegetable-oil cooking spray for the griddle

1 pint blueberries

Powdered sugar for dusting

Warm maple syrup for serving

Preheat the oven to 200°F. Have ready a rimmed baking sheet.

To make the hotcakes, in a bowl, using a rubber spatula, stir together the ricotta, egg yolks, butter, and lemon zest until combined. Sift together the flour, granulated sugar, and salt into the ricotta mixture, and stir until blended.

In another bowl, using an electric mixer set on medium-high speed, whip the egg whites until stiff peaks form. Stir one-fourth of the whites into the ricotta mixture to lighten it, then fold in the remaining whites.

Heat a griddle or large skillet over medium heat. Lightly spray with cooking spray. Using ¼ cup batter for each hotcake, pour the batter onto the griddle, creating hotcakes about 4 inches in diameter and being careful not to crowd the griddle. Cook until bubbles form on the surface and the undersides are golden brown, about 2 minutes. Turn the hotcakes over and cook until the second sides are browned, about 1½ minutes longer. Transfer the hotcakes to the baking sheet and keep warm in the oven. Repeat with the remaining batter.

Arrange the hotcakes on warmed plates, and top with the blueberries. Using a fine-mesh sieve, dust the hotcakes with the powdered sugar, and then sprinkle with lemon zest. Serve immediately and pass the maple syrup at the table.

HONEY ORANGE PANNA COTTA WITH FRESH BERRIES

Although *panna cotta* means "cooked cream" in Italian, the cream is really only heated enough to dissolve the
gelatin that thickens it so it will hold its shape when chilled. With its light texture and creamy profile, this dessert is the perfect
ending to a summer meal, especially when served with your favorite berries. [CHEF ALYSSA KASPAREK]

Serves 6

1 cup whole milk

1 envelope (1 tablespoon) unflavored
   powdered gelatin

3 cups heavy (whipping) cream

⅓ cup honey, preferably orange
   blossom

1 tablespoon sugar

Grated zest of ½ orange

Pinch of fine sea salt

1 vanilla bean, split lengthwise

2 cups assorted berries such as
   raspberries, blueberries, and sliced
   strawberries, in any combination,
   or your favorite single berry
   variety

6 fresh mint sprigs

Pour the milk into a small, heavy-bottomed saucepan. Sprinkle the gelatin over the milk
and let stand until the gelatin softens, about 5 minutes. Place over low heat and heat, stirring
constantly, just until the gelatin dissolves (do not let the milk boil). Stir in the cream, honey,
sugar, orange zest, and salt. Using the tip of a small knife, scrape the seeds from the vanilla
pod into the saucepan, and then add the pod. Cook, stirring constantly, just until the sugar
dissolves. Remove from the heat and let cool for 10 minutes, then remove the vanilla pod
and discard.

Transfer the cream mixture to a 1-quart glass measuring or other pitcher. Divide it evenly
among 6 martini glasses. Cover with plastic wrap and refrigerate until well chilled and set,
at least 6 hours or up to overnight.

Arrange some of the berries on top of each serving, and then garnish each serving with a
mint sprig. Serve chilled.

PEAR AND CURRANT BREAD PUDDING

There is a simple reason why we have more than one bread pudding in this book: everyone loves this comforting dessert. In this version, fresh pears are combined with dried currants and treated to a generous splash of Cognac. [CHEF ROB GIBBS]

Serves 9

3 cups heavy (whipping) cream

1½ cups whole milk

¾ cup granulated sugar

1½ teaspoons vanilla bean paste (see Chef's Note, page 210)

4 tablespoons (½ stick) unsalted butter

3 firm, ripe D'Anjou pears, peeled, cored, and cut into ¼-inch dice

⅓ cup dried currants

3 tablespoons firmly packed brown sugar

3 tablespoons Cognac or other brandy

4 large eggs

6 large egg yolks

1 loaf day-old French bread (1 pound), cut into 1-inch cubes

1 teaspoon ground cinnamon

TOPPING

1 cup heavy (whipping) cream

Homemade or store-bought caramel sauce, warmed

Preheat the oven to 325°F.

In a saucepan over medium heat, combine the cream, milk, and granulated sugar and stir together until the mixture is steaming. Remove from the heat and stir in the vanilla bean paste. Set aside to cool slightly.

In a large skillet over medium heat, melt the butter. Pour 2 tablespoons of the butter into a 9-by-13-by-2-inch baking dish. Brush the melted butter over the bottom and sides of the dish. Set aside.

Add the pears to the butter remaining in the skillet and cook over medium heat, stirring occasionally, until beginning to soften, about 2 minutes. Add the currants and brown sugar and cook, stirring occasionally, until the sugar has melted, about 3 minutes. Remove the skillet from the heat, and carefully pour in the Cognac. Using a wooden spoon, dislodge any browned bits stuck to the pan bottom. Return the pan to medium heat and cook until the Cognac has evaporated, about 1 minute. Remove from the heat and let cool until tepid.

In a large bowl, whisk together the eggs and egg yolks until blended. Gradually whisk in the warm cream mixture.

In a large bowl, combine the bread and the pear mixture and mix together gently. Slowly pour the cream mixture over the bread and fruit, and press down on the bread to help it absorb the custard completely. Transfer the mixture to the prepared baking dish, gently smooth it out, and then sprinkle evenly with the cinnamon. Cover the pan with aluminum foil.

Bake for 40 minutes. Remove the foil and continue baking until evenly browned and a knife inserted in the center of the pudding comes out clean, about 25 minutes more. Transfer to a wire rack and let cool until warm.

To make the Topping, in a chilled bowl, using the stand mixer fitted with the whisk attachment or a handheld mixer, whip the cream on medium-high speed until it holds firm peaks. Cover and refrigerate until ready to use.

Serve the bread pudding warm with the whipped cream and caramel sauce.

BLUE CHEESE WITH PEAR VANILLA MARMALADE

Nothing does the job of tempering the sharpness of blue cheese better than fruit, especially firm, juicy pears. Here, the pears are simmered into a thick homemade marmalade, the perfect counterpoint to the distinctively flavored cheese. Serve this combination as an appetizer with peppery lahvosh crackers, or as a sweet-and-savory dessert with plain crackers. [DAVID KIM]

Serves 4 to 6

PEAR MARMALADE

5 ripe Bartlett pears, peeled, cored, and cut into ½-inch dice

1 cup sugar

Grated zest of ½ lemon

2 tablespoons fresh lemon juice

Grated zest of ¼ orange

2 tablespoons fresh orange juice

2 vanilla beans, split lengthwise

1 tablespoon unsalted butter

½ pound blue cheese, preferably Point Reyes Blue (see Chef's Note), at room temperature

Crisp crackers for serving

To make the Pear Marmalade, in a heavy-bottomed saucepan, combine the pears, sugar, lemon zest and juice, and orange zest and juice. Using the tip of a small knife, scrape the seeds from the vanilla pods into the saucepan; discard the pods or save for another use. Cook over medium-low heat, stirring often, until the pears are tender and translucent and the liquid is thick and syrupy, about 45 minutes. Remove from the heat, stir in the butter, and let cool. (The marmalade can be made up to 1 week ahead, cooled, covered, and refrigerated. Bring to room temperature before using.)

Place the blue cheese on a platter. Spoon some of the marmalade over half of the cheese, and place the remaining marmalade in a small serving bowl. (This way, guests can serve themselves cheese with or without the preserves.) Serve with the crackers.

CHEF'S NOTE: *From Roquefort to Gorgonzola, Maytag to Danish, there are a lot of choices for blue cheese. But one variety stands out: Point Reyes Blue from Tomales Bay in California. The happy combination of contented Holstein cows grazing on lush green pastures, coastal fog, and salty Pacific breezes makes this a remarkable creamy, full-flavored blue cheese.*

ORANGE DATE AND CILANTRO SALAD

This salad, a version of which I enjoyed on a trip to the Napa Valley, clearly illustrates why California is so famous for its produce. It is about texture as much as it is about flavor: crunchy lettuce, juicy oranges, and chewy dates, all held together with a bracing cilantro vinaigrette. It is a particularly nice addition to a menu served alfresco. [DAVID KIM]

Serves 4

CILANTRO VINAIGRETTE

¼ cup Champagne or white wine vinegar

3 tablespoons honey

¼ cup firmly packed chopped fresh cilantro

¼ teaspoon ground coriander

½ teaspoon ground cumin

¼ teaspoon sweet paprika, preferably Hungarian

¾ cup extra-virgin olive oil

Kosher salt

Freshly ground black pepper

4 large navel oranges

½ red onion, thinly sliced

3 romaine lettuce hearts, chopped

10 pitted dates, cut lengthwise into sixths

To make the Cilantro Vinaigrette, in a blender, combine the vinegar, honey, cilantro, coriander, cumin, and paprika. With the machine running, add the oil in a thin, steady stream to form an emulsion. Season to taste with salt and pepper. Set aside.

Grate the zest of 1 orange and set aside to use for garnish. Working with 1 orange at a time, cut a slice off the top and bottom to reveal the flesh. Stand the orange upright on the work surface. Using a serrated knife, cut off the thick peel in strips, following the contour of the fruit and removing all of the white pith and membrane. Holding the fruit over a bowl, cut along both sides of each segment to free it from the thin membrane and let the segments and any juice fall into the bowl. Squeeze the juice from the membranes into the bowl. Drain the segments in a sieve, capturing the juice in a small bowl. Add the onion to the orange juice and set aside to marinate for at least 10 minutes or up to 1 hour.

To assemble the salad, drain the onion, discarding the juice. In a large bowl, combine the lettuce, dates, orange segments, and onion. Drizzle with the vinaigrette and toss to coat all the ingredients evenly.

Divide the salad evenly among chilled salad bowls, building up the height of each in the center. Sprinkle with the orange zest and serve immediately.

CHEF'S NOTE: *Chilled bowls or plates keep salads cool and crisp. Simply pop them into the freezer for about 5 minutes. It's a small touch but easy to accomplish, and it can make the big difference when serving a salad on a hot day.*

BANANA CRÈME BRÛLÉE WITH RASPBERRIES

Crème brûlée is both easy to make and impressive, which largely accounts for its popularity on restaurant menus. Chefs also love it because it allows for creativity in flavoring the custard and devising interesting garnishes beyond the familiar sugar crust. Here, the topping is caramelized bananas. The warm, sugared banana provides another layer of flavor and texture to the creamy custard, and a scattering of raspberries adds bright color and a tart accent. [CHEF MICHAEL LYLE]

Serves 8

4 cups heavy (whipping) cream

1 cup sugar, plus more for sprinkling

1 vanilla bean, split lengthwise

10 large egg yolks

2 bananas

1 pint raspberries

8 fresh mint sprigs

CHEF'S NOTE: *Eggs are quite delicate, and if you heat them beyond 180°F, you could end up with scrambled eggs. When making the custard, gradually add the hot cream to the eggs, whisking constantly to keep the eggs in motion. This technique, in which you are slowly equalizing two opposite temperatures to a common ground, is called tempering.*

Preheat the oven to 300°F. Place eight ¾-cup shallow crème brûlée dishes or ramekins, not touching, in a large roasting pan.

In a heavy-bottomed saucepan over low heat, combine the cream, sugar, and vanilla bean and bring to a simmer, stirring to dissolve the sugar. Remove from the heat, cover, and let steep for 10 minutes. Remove the vanilla bean and, using the tip of a small knife, scrape the seeds from the vanilla pod into the saucepan; discard the pod. In a bowl, whisk the egg yolks until they begin to turn pale. Whisking constantly, slowly whisk in the hot cream.

Ladle the custard into the dishes. Cover the pan with aluminum foil, but leave 1 corner open. Carefully place the pan in the oven, with the uncovered corner facing you. Using a pitcher or kettle, add hot tap water to the pan to come halfway up the sides of the dishes. Close and tighten the foil at the open corner.

Bake the custards until they are set and do not quiver when a dish is gently shaken (uncover the pan carefully, as hot steam will escape), about 50 minutes.

Carefully remove the pan from the oven and remove the foil. Remove the custards from the water and let cool completely. Cover each dish with plastic wrap and refrigerate until completely chilled, at least 4 hours or up to 1 day.

When ready to serve, preheat the broiler.

Peel the bananas and cut them into thin slices. Arrange an equal number of the banana slices on top of each custard. Sprinkle about 2 teaspoons sugar over each custard. Place the custards on the broiler rack about 6 inches from the heat source, and broil until the sugar is melted and caramelized and a thin, glasslike coating has formed on top, 1 to 2 minutes. Alternatively, use a kitchen torch to caramelize the sugar, working in slow, steady passes to caramelize evenly. Let cool slightly.

Garnish each crème brûlée with some raspberries and a mint sprig. Serve immediately.

RASPBERRY WHITE CHOCOLATE CHEESECAKE

Every chef (and home cook, for that matter) needs a special dessert that he or she can serve and be
guaranteed accolades. This luscious cheesecake is mine. One of its many positive attributes is that it must be made ahead of time,
which takes last-minute pressure off of the host or hostess. [MICHAEL THOMS]

Serves 14

CRUST

⅔ cup (about 3 ounces) slivered
blanched almonds

1⅓ cups graham cracker crumbs
(about 16 crackers)

6 tablespoons (¾ stick) unsalted
butter, melted

1½ pints fresh raspberries

FILLING

2 cups (12 ounces) white chocolate
morsels

3 packages (8 ounces each) cream
cheese, at room temperature

½ cup sugar

3 large eggs, at room temperature

1 teaspoon pure vanilla extract

Preheat the oven to 315°F. Lightly butter a 10-inch round springform pan.

To make the Crust, in a food processor fitted with the metal chopping blade, pulse the almonds until finely ground. Add the cracker crumbs and pulse to combine. Add the butter and pulse until the mixture is evenly moistened. Transfer the crumb mixture to the prepared pan and firmly and evenly press it onto the bottom of the pan. Arrange a single layer of the raspberries, stem sides down, over the crust.

To make the Filling, bring 1 inch of water to a bare simmer in the bottom of a double boiler or a saucepan. Place the white chocolate morsels in the top of the double boiler or in a heatproof bowl and place over (not touching) the simmering water. Heat, stirring occasionally, until the chocolate has melted and is smooth. (Take care that the water isn't too hot, as white chocolate scorches easily.) Remove from the heat and let the chocolate cool until tepid but still fluid.

Using a food processor fitted with the metal chopping blade, combine the cream cheese and sugar and process until light in texture. With the machine running, add the eggs, one at a time, stopping to scrape down the sides of the bowl as needed. Add the melted chocolate and vanilla and process until thoroughly combined and smooth, stopping to scrape down the sides of the bowl as needed. Pour the filling evenly over the raspberries and smooth the top. Rap the pan against the counter to expel any trapped air.

Bake the cheesecake until its edges have risen and the filling seems set when the pan is rapped, 1 hour to 1 hour and 10 minutes. Transfer to a wire rack and let cool completely in the pan. Cover with plastic wrap and refrigerate until chilled, at least 4 hours or up to 24 hours.

To serve, run a thin-bladed knife around the inside of the pan to release the sides of the cheesecake, and then remove the sides of the pan. Cut the cheesecake into wedges, dipping the knife blade into hot water before each cut and wiping it clean after each cut. Serve chilled.

CHEF'S NOTE: *To create a raspberry swirl for this cheesecake, in a small bowl, mix together ¼ cup of the batter and 2 tablespoons raspberry preserves. Fill the crust with the plain batter as directed, and then drizzle the raspberry batter on top. Swirl a dinner knife through the batters to create a marbled effect.*

BRAISED VEAL SHANKS IN MERLOT FIG SAUCE

Forget all of the talk about "fast and easy cooking." Slow cooking has become wildly popular in the last few years as cooks rediscovered the rich, intense flavors it produces. This recipe infuses the Merlot, with its raspberry jam note, and the fragrant herbs right into the succulent veal. If your guests ask what the secret ingredient in the sauce is, you can tell them figs . . . or keep it to yourself. Serve alongside Herb Garden Risotto (page 21) for a hearty meal. [CHEF DANIEL WOOD]

Serves 6

1 cup all-purpose flour

6 meaty, center-cut veal shanks (about 4 pounds total), cut 1½ inches thick

Kosher salt

Freshly ground black pepper

¼ cup plus 2 tablespoons extra-virgin olive oil

1 large yellow onion, chopped

1 large carrot, peeled and chopped

2 celery stalks, chopped

6 cloves garlic, finely chopped

1½ teaspoons finely chopped fresh thyme

½ teaspoon finely chopped fresh rosemary

1 bay leaf

2 cups Merlot wine

2½ cups low-sodium chicken broth

12 dried Mission figs, roughly chopped

2 tablespoons unsalted butter

Preheat the oven to 325°F.

Put the flour into a shallow dish. Season the veal shanks all over with 2 teaspoons salt and 1 teaspoon pepper. Coat the veal evenly with the flour, shaking off the excess.

In a very large Dutch oven over medium-high heat, heat ¼ cup of the oil until very hot but not smoking. Working in batches to avoid crowding, add the veal and cook, turning occasionally, until browned on all sides, about 10 minutes. Transfer to a platter. Wipe out the pot with paper towels.

Return the pot to medium-high heat and add the remaining 2 tablespoons oil. Add the onion, carrot, celery, garlic, thyme, rosemary, and bay leaf and cook, stirring often, until the vegetables begin to brown, about 12 minutes. Season to taste with salt and pepper.

Add the Merlot, increase the heat to high, and bring to a boil, scraping up the browned bits. Boil until the wine reduces by half, about 10 minutes. Stir in the broth and add the figs. Return the veal to the pot and bring back to a simmer. Cover tightly.

Transfer the pot to the oven and cook until the veal is very tender, about 1 hour and 45 minutes. Using a slotted spoon, transfer the veal to a deep platter and cover with aluminum foil to keep warm.

Discard the bay leaf. Skim any fat from the top of the cooking liquid. Working in batches, transfer the cooking liquid and vegetables to a blender, taking care not to fill the jar more than half full. With the lid vented, process until smooth and transfer to a saucepan. If the sauce seems too thick, thin with a little water. Warm the sauce gently over low heat, whisk in the butter, and season with salt and pepper.

Pour the sauce over the veal and serve immediately.

HONEY-GLAZED DUCK BREAST WITH PANCETTA

This dish was created with a specific purpose: to hit as many flavor notes as possible with a minimum of ingredients. Here, earthy port, sweet honey, smoky-salty pancetta, and tart blood oranges work together in harmony to enhance the meaty flavor of the duck breasts. Look for duck breast halves at specialty markets. [CHEF ROB GIBBS]

Serves 4

2 cups tawny port

½-pound piece pancetta, rind removed and cut into ¼-inch dice

4 large blood oranges

4 boneless duck breast halves (about 7 ounces each)

1 teaspoon kosher salt

½ teaspoon freshly ground black pepper

¼ cup honey, preferably clover

CHEF'S NOTE: *Pancetta is traditionally salt-cured pork belly (the same cut as bacon), usually rolled into a thick cylinder. You'll find it at Italian delicatessens and most supermarkets.*

In a heavy-bottomed saucepan over high heat, bring the port to a boil. Reduce the heat to medium and cook at a steady simmer until the port is syrupy and reduced to about ½ cup, about 25 minutes. Let cool completely.

Meanwhile, in a large nonstick skillet over medium heat, cook the pancetta, stirring occasionally, until crisp and browned, about 10 minutes. Using a slotted spoon, transfer to paper towels to drain. Set aside.

Working with 1 orange at a time, cut a slice off the top and bottom to reveal the flesh. Stand the orange upright on the work surface. Using a serrated knife, cut off the thick peel in strips, following the contour of the fruit and removing all of the white pith and membrane. Holding the fruit over a bowl, cut along both sides of each segment to free it from the thin membrane and let the segments fall into the bowl. Cover and refrigerate until ready to serve.

Score the duck skin in a crisscross pattern, taking care not to cut into the flesh. (This allows the skin to release more fat while cooking, which in turn makes it crispier.) Season the duck breasts on both sides with the salt and pepper. Heat a very large skillet over medium-high heat. Add the breasts, skin side down, and cook until the undersides are golden brown, about 5 minutes. Turn the duck over and cook until the second sides are lightly browned, about 3 minutes longer. Transfer the duck to a platter and pour off and discard the fat from the pan.

Return the pan to medium-high heat. When it is hot, return the duck, skin side up, to the pan and brush the skin with the honey. Cook until the duck feels only slightly resilient when pressed in the center (or an instant-read thermometer inserted horizontally into the center of a breast reads 135°F for medium), about 4 minutes more. Transfer the duck to a carving board and let rest for 5 minutes.

To serve, arrange equal amounts of crisp pancetta in the center of warmed dinner plates. Using a sharp knife held at a slight diagonal, cut each duck breast across the grain into ½-inch-thick slices. Arrange the duck slices on the plates, fanning them over the pancetta. Drizzle the reduced port over the duck breasts and onto the plates. Garnish each serving with an equal amount of the blood orange segments and serve immediately.

CHOCOLATE AND VANILLA

ROASTED PINEAPPLE WITH VANILLA "SPIKES"

I remember seeing a photograph of this intriguing dessert in a cookbook long ago (though I don't remember which one), and this is my attempt to re-create it. The pineapple was trimmed of its leaves, so the whole thing looked like a glossy, golden Sputnik. This recipe is as simple as it gets, with only three ingredients, yet everyone who has tasted it has declared it "Awesome!" Buy a pineapple tagged "jet fresh," which means it was left to ripen naturally on the plant and not harvested prematurely like most pineapples in the market. You won't find a sweeter pineapple anywhere. [CHEF MICHAEL NORTHERN]

Serves 6 to 8

¾ cup homemade or store-bought caramel sauce

1 ripe pineapple, preferably jet fresh

4 vanilla beans, split lengthwise, then cut into thirds to make 24 pieces total

Vanilla bean ice cream for serving

CHEF'S NOTE: *There is no reason to toss out the vanilla-bean segments used in this recipe (they are a luxury). Instead, use them to make a pineapple-and-vanilla-infused vodka. In a 1-quart jar, combine the vanilla pieces and 2 cups fresh pineapple chunks. Add enough vodka to cover the pineapple and vanilla completely. Cover and refrigerate for at least 1 week before serving. The pineapple-vanilla vodka mixture will keep for up to 2 months. To use, strain off only what you need.*

Position a rack in the lower third of the oven (with enough room left above to clear the height of the pineapple and its trimmed top) and preheat to 450°F. In a small bowl, mix together the caramel sauce and 2 tablespoons water; set aside.

Lay the pineapple on its side. Using a sharp knife, and cutting away from you, carve the leaves into a cone shape about 3 inches high. Cut off the bottom of the pineapple so the fruit will stand straight up. Stand the pineapple upright and carefully pare away the outer skin. Remove the "eyes" by grooving channels into the pineapple, working on a diagonal, like the stripes on a barber pole.

Using a paring knife, cut 24 equally spaced 2-inch-deep slits all over the pineapple. Insert a vanilla piece into each slit, leaving ½ inch of the vanilla visible. Wrap aluminum foil around the trimmed pineapple leaves to protect them in the oven. Stand the pineapple upright in a 9-inch round cake pan. Brush the pineapple with some of the caramel sauce.

Roast the pineapple for 15 minutes. Reduce the temperature to 400°F. Baste again with the caramel sauce and continue roasting, brushing the pineapple with the caramel sauce at 10-minute intervals, until the pineapple is nicely browned and easily pierced with a long metal or wooden skewer, about 60 minutes more.

Carefully remove the pineapple from the oven and let cool for about 15 minutes. Reserve the sauce that has collected in the pan. Using a wide, stiff spatula, transfer the pineapple to a serving platter. Unwrap the foil from the top.

To serve, spoon the accumulated pan drippings over the pineapple and present it at the table in all of its spiky glory. Return to the kitchen and remove the vanilla-bean segments. Transfer the pineapple to a cutting board. Cut off and discard the top, and then cut the pineapple lengthwise into 6 wedges. Cut the solid core away from each wedge, and then cut the wedges into chunks. Scoop the ice cream into individual bowls, and top with the warm pineapple chunks and pan juices. Serve immediately.

BOSTON CREAM PIE

Why choose between vanilla and chocolate when you can have both? Perhaps that's the reason why this old-fashioned dessert continues to have legions of fans. It isn't actually a pie, but a cake harking back to the time when most cakes were baked in pie pans. No matter what you call it, it has been a mainstay at the Omni Parker House Hotel in Boston since 1855. [DAVID KIM]

Serves 10

CAKE

6 tablespoons (¾ stick) unsalted butter, plus more for the pans

1 cup cake flour, sifted, plus more for the pans

⅛ teaspoon fine sea salt

6 large eggs, at room temperature

¾ cup sugar

1 teaspoon pure vanilla extract

½ teaspoon grated lemon zest

VANILLA CUSTARD FILLING

6 large egg yolks

½ cup sugar

⅓ cup cornstarch

2 cups whole milk

3 tablespoons unsalted butter, cubed

1 teaspoon pure vanilla extract

¾ cup heavy (whipping) cream

GLAZE

½ cup heavy (whipping) cream

4 ounces high-quality bittersweet chocolate, coarsely chopped

½ teaspoon pure vanilla extract

To make the Cake, preheat the oven to 350°F. Lightly butter the bottom and sides of two 9-inch round cake pans. Line the bottoms with waxed paper. Dust the bottoms and sides with flour and tap out the excess.

In a bowl, sift together the flour and salt and set aside. In a small saucepan over medium heat, melt the butter. Pour into a medium bowl and set aside to cool until tepid.

Bring 1 inch of water to a simmer in a saucepan. In the bowl of a stand mixer or in a large heatproof bowl, whisk together the eggs and sugar until blended. Place the bowl over (not touching) the simmering water. Whisking constantly, heat until the sugar has dissolved and the eggs are warm to the touch.

Using the whisk attachment of the stand mixer or a handheld mixer, beat the egg mixture on high speed until it triples in volume and is very light and fluffy, about 3 minutes for a stand mixer or 5 minutes for a handheld mixer. On low speed, mix in the vanilla and lemon zest. Detach the bowl from the stand mixer, if using. Sift one-third of the flour mixture over the eggs and fold in with a rubber spatula. Repeat with the remaining flour in 2 equal additions.

Stir about 1 cup of the batter into the tepid butter, and then pour the combined mixtures back into the batter and fold together until incorporated. Divide the batter evenly between the prepared pans and smooth the tops with the spatula.

Bake the cake layers until a wooden toothpick inserted in the center of each cake comes out clean, about 22 minutes. Let the cakes cool in the pans on wire racks for 10 minutes. Run a thin-bladed knife around the inside of each pan to release the cake sides. Invert a rack on top of 1 cake, invert the cake and rack together, and then carefully lift off the pan. Peel off and discard the waxed paper. Turn the cake layer right side up. Repeat with the second cake layer. Let cool completely.

To make the Vanilla Custard Filling, fill a large bowl with a mixture of ice cubes and water to use for cooling the custard and set aside. In a bowl, whisk together the egg yolks, sugar, and cornstarch. In a heavy-bottomed saucepan over medium heat, bring the milk to a gentle simmer. Whisking constantly, gradually add about half of the hot milk to the egg yolk mixture. Whisk the combined mixtures back into the saucepan and cook over medium-low heat, stirring constantly with a wooden spatula, until the custard comes to a full boil. Reduce the heat to low so the mixture bubbles steadily and cook, stirring constantly, for 2 minutes. Remove from the heat, add the butter and vanilla, and whisk until the butter melts.

Strain the custard through a fine-mesh sieve into a bowl. Cover with plastic wrap pressed directly on the surface, and pierce the plastic with a few slits to allow steam to escape. Place the bowl in the ice-water bath. Let stand, adding more ice to the water as needed to keep the water ice-cold, until the custard is chilled, about 1 hour.

In a chilled bowl, using an electric mixer on high speed, whip the heavy cream until soft peaks form. Using a rubber spatula, stir one-third of the whipped cream into the chilled custard to lighten it, creating a smooth mixture. Fold in the remaining cream just until incorporated. Cover and refrigerate the filling until ready to use.

To make the Glaze, in a small saucepan over medium heat, bring the cream to a simmer. Remove from the heat and add the chocolate. Let stand until the chocolate melts, about 3 minutes. Add the vanilla and whisk gently (so you don't create bubbles that will mar the glaze) until the chocolate melts. Set the glaze aside to cool and thicken slightly.

Use a long serrated knife to cut each cake layer in half horizontally to make 4 layers total. Set aside 1 top layer to serve as the top of the pie. Place 1 of the remaining cake rounds, cut side up, on a serving platter. Spread one-third of the filling over the cake, then top with another cake layer. Spread with one-half of the remaining filling, and top with another layer. Spread with the remaining filling, and place the reserved top layer, smooth side up, on top.

Pour the warm glaze over the top of the cake. Using a metal icing spatula or offset spatula, smooth the glaze over the top, letting any excess glaze drip down the sides. Refrigerate for at least 3 hours or up to 24 hours before serving; bring to room temperature before serving.

CHEF'S NOTE: *The conventional rule is never boil a custard or the eggs will curdle. When making a custard filling, however, the cornstarch acts to insulate the egg yolks. In fact, if the custard does not come to a boil, it will thin out and not thicken when chilled. Just keep stirring the custard, being careful to run the wooden spatula over the entire bottom of the pan so the custard doesn't scorch.*

DARK CHOCOLATE BLACKOUT CAKE

A chocolate lover's dream, this infamous cake combines pudding, cake, and ganache frosting with a thick
coating of cake crumbs. Ebinger's, the Brooklyn bakery that invented it, was shuttered decades ago, so it was left to me
and my wife to re-create the popular cake. [CHEF CORY GOODMAN]

Serves 16

CAKE

1 cup (2 sticks) unsalted butter, at room temperature, plus more for the pans

2 cups all-purpose flour, plus more for the pans

¾ cup unsweetened natural cocoa powder (not Dutch processed)

1 teaspoon baking powder

1 teaspoon baking soda

1 teaspoon fine sea salt

2 cups sugar

3 large eggs, at room temperature

1½ teaspoons pure vanilla extract

1 cup buttermilk, at room temperature

1 cup strong brewed coffee, at room temperature

GANACHE

2 cups heavy (whipping) cream

3 cups (18 ounces) semisweet chocolate morsels

To make the Cake, preheat the oven to 350°F. Lightly butter the bottom and sides of two 9-inch round cake pans. Line the bottoms with waxed paper. Dust the bottoms and sides with flour and tap out the excess.

In a bowl, sift together the flour, cocoa, baking powder, baking soda, and salt. In a bowl, using an electric mixer on high speed, beat together the butter and sugar until the mixture is light and fluffy, about 3 minutes, stopping to scrape down the sides of the bowl as needed. Reduce the speed to medium and add the eggs, one at a time, beating well after each addition. Beat in the vanilla. Add the flour mixture in 3 equal additions alternately with the buttermilk in 2 equal additions, beginning and ending with the flour mixture and mixing well after each addition. Stop to scrape down the sides of the bowl as needed with a rubber spatula. Add the coffee and mix until just blended. Divide the batter evenly between the prepared pans and smooth the tops with the spatula.

Bake the cake layers until a wooden toothpick inserted in the center of each cake comes out clean, 30 to 35 minutes. Let the cakes cool in the pans on wire racks for 10 minutes. Run a thin-bladed knife around the inside of each pan to release the cake sides. Invert a rack on top of 1 cake, invert the cake and rack together, and then carefully lift off the pan. Peel off and discard the waxed paper. Turn the cake layer right side up. Repeat with the second cake layer. Let cool completely.

To make the Ganache, in a saucepan over medium heat, bring the cream to a simmer. Remove from the heat and add the chocolate morsels. Let stand until the chocolate melts, about 3 minutes. Whisk gently until the mixture is smooth. Transfer to a bowl. Let stand at room temperature, stirring occasionally, until cooled and slightly thickened, about 2 hours. (The ganache can be made up to 1 day ahead, cooled, covered, and stored at room temperature.)

To make the Pudding, fill a large bowl with a mixture of ice cubes and water to use for cooling the pudding and set aside. In a heavy-bottomed saucepan, sift together the sugar, cornstarch, cocoa, and salt. Gradually whisk in the milk until the dry ingredients are dissolved. Add the chocolate morsels. Place over medium-high heat and cook, whisking constantly, until the mixture is smooth and boiling, about 7 minutes. Remove from the heat and whisk in the butter, 1 tablespoon at a time.

continued >

PUDDING

¼ cup sugar

2 tablespoons cornstarch

2 tablespoons unsweetened natural cocoa powder (not Dutch processed)

¼ teaspoon fine sea salt

1½ cups whole milk

1 cup (6 ounces) semisweet chocolate morsels

2 tablespoons unsalted butter, at room temperature

Pour the pudding into a bowl and cover with plastic wrap pressed directly onto the surface. Pierce the plastic with a few slits to allow steam to escape. Place the bowl in the ice-water bath. Let stand, adding more ice to the water as needed to keep the water ice-cold, until the pudding is chilled and spreadable, about 1 hour.

To assemble the cake, use a long serrated knife to cut each cake layer in half horizontally to make 4 layers total. Break 1 layer into pieces, and transfer to a food processor fitted with the metal chopping blade. Pulse until reduced to fine cake crumbs. Spread on a baking sheet and set aside.

Line a baking sheet with waxed paper. Place a cake layer, cut side up, on a 9-inch cardboard cake round (or use the base of a tart pan or springform pan). Using an offset spatula, spread half of the pudding on the layer. Top with a second layer, smooth side up, and spread with the remaining pudding. Place the third layer on top, smooth side up, and press gently to even out cake and set layers together. (Put the cake on its round on the lined baking sheet, for catching the ganache).

Using an offset spatula, frost the top and then the sides of the cake with the ganache. The ganache will be slightly loose and will pour off the sides of the cake, so you may need to ice the sides several times to get good coverage. Don't worry if you can't cover the sides perfectly, as you will be covering the ganache with cake crumbs.

Refrigerate the cake until the ganache is slightly set, about 5 minutes. Remove the cake from the refrigerator. Use one hand to hold the cake over the baking sheet of crumbs. Use your other hand to press the crumbs onto the top and sides of the cake, letting any crumbs that don't stick fall back onto the baking sheet. Refrigerate to set the crumb coating, about 2 hours. (The cake can be made 1 day ahead, covered loosely with plastic wrap, and refrigerated.)

Remove the cake from the refrigerator 1 hour before serving. Place the cake on a cake plate. Cut into wedges to serve.

CHEF'S NOTE: *There are two kinds of cocoa powder, and they are quite different. Some cocoa powders, especially European brands, are treated with alkali to reduce their acidity and to deepen their cocoa color. The inventor of the process was from the Netherlands, so these products are usually labeled Dutch-processed cocoa. Natural cocoa powder, such as the familiar Hershey's in the dark brown box, has not been treated, which means it is more acidic and is the cocoa to use when the a batter recipe includes an alkali, like baking soda. The acidic and alkaline ingredients in the batter create a chemical reaction that makes the cake rise. If you use Dutch-processed cocoa in a batter that includes baking soda, the cake might not rise. Batters with baking powder will work fine with natural or Dutch-processed cocoa powder.*

KILLER CHOCOLATE BROWNIES

Gail LaLumiere contributed Neighborhood Brownies to the first Nordstrom's cookbook, *Friends and Family.*
Here, the recipe is perked up with the addition of macadamia nuts and chunks of white chocolate. [CHEF MICHAEL NORTHERN]

Makes 16 brownies

Vegetable-oil cooking spray for preparing the pan

¾ cup (1½ sticks) unsalted butter, cut up

3 ounces unsweetened chocolate, finely chopped

1½ cups sugar

¼ teaspoon kosher salt

3 large eggs, lightly beaten

¾ cup all-purpose flour

1 bar (4 ounces) high-quality semisweet chocolate, cut into ½-inch chunks

¾ cup (3½ ounces) macadamia nuts, toasted (see Chef's Note, page 207)

1 bar (4 ounces) high-quality white chocolate, cut into ½-inch chunks

Preheat the oven to 350°F. Spray a 9-inch square baking pan with cooking spray.

In a saucepan over low heat, melt the butter. Remove from the heat and add the unsweetened chocolate. Let stand until the chocolate has softened, then whisk until smooth. Whisk in the sugar and salt and let cool slightly.

Whisk the eggs into the chocolate mixture. Add the flour and stir until smooth with a wooden spoon or rubber spatula. (Do not use a whisk because the batter will stick to the wires.) Add the semisweet chocolate chunks and macadamia nuts and stir until evenly distributed in the batter. Spread the batter evenly in the prepared pan.

Bake the brownie until it has risen somewhat and a thin crust has formed on top, about 12 minutes. Remove the pan from the oven. Distributing them evenly, carefully press the white chocolate chunks into the thin crust so that some of each chunk is still peeking through the top. Return the pan to the oven. Continue baking until the center of the brownie has risen slightly and the white chocolate is tinged beige, about 18 minutes more. You want the brownies to be very fudgy and moist, so it is better to underbake them than to overbake them. Transfer to a wire rack and let cool completely.

Cut into 2-inch squares and serve. Store any leftover brownies in an airtight container at room temperature for up to 2 days.

CHEF'S NOTE: *These brownies are chocolate and more chocolate, so use your favorite brand. To get the right thickness for the chunks, use chocolate bars, not blocks. And don't be tempted to add the white chocolate to the batter with the semisweet chocolate. White chocolate is delicate and might scorch if baked for the entire time.*

MOCHA BREAD PUDDING

Chocoholics, I give you fair warning: once you try this unusual recipe, bread pudding will never be the same for you again! Chocolate and coffee bring out the best in each other, as this recipe proves. As for the bread, use a middle-of-the-road French or Italian loaf with a firm crumb, not a rustic sourdough with a crisp crust. [CHEF RICHARD VENZOR]

Serves 6 to 8

Unsalted butter for the baking dish

1 cup strong brewed coffee

3 cups heavy (whipping) cream

1 cup whole milk

1 cup granulated sugar

½ cup firmly packed light brown sugar

4 large eggs

6 large egg yolks

1 loaf French bread (1 pound), preferably day old (see Chef's Note), cut into 1-inch pieces

8 ounces high-quality bittersweet chocolate, coarsely chopped

Powdered sugar for dusting

Preheat the oven to 325°F. Lightly butter a 9-by-13-by-2-inch baking dish.

In a small saucepan over high heat, boil the coffee until reduced to 2 tablespoons. Remove from the heat and set aside.

In a heavy-bottomed saucepan over medium heat, combine the cream, milk, and granulated and brown sugars and bring to a simmer, stirring to dissolve the sugar. Remove from the heat and let cool slightly.

In a large bowl, whisk together the eggs and egg yolks until blended. Whisking constantly, gradually add the hot cream mixture. Whisk in the reduced coffee. Add the bread and stir gently to coat with the custard. Let stand, stirring occasionally, until the bread has absorbed most of the custard, about 20 minutes. Fold in the chocolate. Spread in the prepared baking dish and cover with aluminum foil.

Bake the pudding until it looks set around the edges, about 40 minutes. Remove the foil and continue baking until a knife inserted in the center of the pudding comes out clean, about 15 minutes more. Remove from the oven and let cool for 10 minutes.

Using a fine-mesh sieve, sift powdered sugar over the top of the pudding. Serve warm.

CHEF'S NOTE: *If the bread isn't day old, cut it into pieces, spread on rimmed baking sheets, and bake in a preheated 300°F oven until the edges begin to crisp, about 10 minutes. Let cool completely before adding to the custard.*

DOUBLE CHOCOLATE POT DE CRÈME

These dense, silky, rich custards will be the highlight of any dinner party. There is nothing to mask the flavor of the chocolate here, so buy the finest your budget can afford. You will get the best of both worlds by mixing bittersweet and milk chocolates. A touch of orange liqueur adds a subtle perfume. [CHEF JONATHAN ROHLAND]

Serves 6

4 ounces high-quality bittersweet chocolate, preferably with a 66% cacao content (such as Valrhona pur Caraibe), coarsely chopped

3 ounces high-quality milk chocolate, preferably with a 40% cacao content (such as Valrhona Guanaja), coarsely chopped

1⅓ cups heavy (whipping) cream

⅔ cup whole milk

3 tablespoons sugar

Pinch of kosher salt

6 large egg yolks

¼ cup orange liqueur such as Grand Marnier

GARNISH

½ cup heavy (whipping) cream

Chocolate shavings (see Chef's Note)

½ pint fresh raspberries

Preheat the oven to 300°F. Place six ¾-cup ramekins, not touching, in a large roasting pan.

In a heatproof bowl, combine the bittersweet and milk chocolates. In a saucepan over medium-high heat, combine the cream, milk, sugar, and salt and bring to a boil, stirring often. Pour the hot cream mixture over the chocolates. Let stand until the chocolates melt, about 3 minutes. Whisk gently until the mixture is smooth.

In a large bowl, whisk together the egg yolks and liqueur until well blended. Gradually whisk in the warm chocolate mixture. Let stand for a few minutes to allow the bubbles on the surface to dissipate.

Using a ladle, carefully divide the chocolate mixture evenly among the ramekins—they will be quite full. Cover the pan with aluminum foil, but leave 1 corner open. Pierce the foil in a few spots to vent the steam during baking. Carefully place the pan in the oven, with the uncovered corner facing you. Using a pitcher or kettle, add hot tap water to the pan to come 1 inch up the sides of the ramekins. Close and tighten the foil at the open corner.

Bake until the center of a custard jiggles only slightly when the dish is gently shaken (uncover the pan carefully, as hot steam will escape), 35 to 40 minutes.

Carefully remove the pan from the oven. Discard the foil. Let the custards cool in the pan for 20 minutes. Remove the ramekins from the pan and wipe the sides clean. Let cool completely.

Cover each ramekin with plastic wrap. Refrigerate until chilled, at least 4 hours or up to 1 day.

To serve, in a chilled bowl, whisk the cream until firm peaks form. Put a dollop of whipped cream on each custard. Top with chocolate shavings and a few raspberries. Serve chilled.

CHEF'S NOTE: *Chocolate shavings are an easy way to decorate your favorite chocolate desserts. Start with a block of chocolate that weighs at least 6 ounces. The chocolate should be at warm room temperature. If it is too cold, the shavings will shatter, rather than curl. Place the chocolate near a warm stove for about 30 minutes, or microwave on low power for 10 seconds. Then, draw a vegetable peeler over the chocolate, letting the shavings fall onto a piece of waxed paper. Refrigerate the shavings until ready to use.*

GERMAN CHOCOLATE CAKE

The German chocolate cake of my childhood is one reason why I became a pastry chef. After experimenting with several different recipes, I decided this one is the best. The coconut-pecan frosting is well known, and well loved, but the addition of chocolate-vanilla cookie crumbs puts this version over the top. This wonderful cake is served at all of our family gatherings. [CHEF JENNY-LYNN FISCHER]

Serves 12

CAKE

Unsalted butter for the pans

2 cups all-purpose flour, plus more for the pans

1 cup sugar

1 cup mayonnaise

1 cup warm water

1 large egg, at room temperature

¼ cup unsweetened natural cocoa powder (not Dutch processed)

2 teaspoons baking soda

1 teaspoon pure vanilla extract

FROSTING

1 can (12 ounces) evaporated milk

1½ cups sugar

¾ cup (1½ sticks) unsalted butter, cut up

4 large egg yolks, lightly beaten

2 teaspoons pure vanilla extract

¼ teaspoon kosher salt

1 package (7 ounces) sweetened flaked coconut

2 cups (8 ounces) pecans, toasted (see Chef's Note) and coarsely chopped

12 cream-filled chocolate sandwich cookies

To make the Cake, preheat the oven to 350°F. Lightly butter the bottom and sides of two 8-inch round cake pans. Line the bottoms with waxed paper. Dust the bottom and sides of the pans with flour and tap out the excess.

In a bowl, using a handheld mixer on medium speed, beat together the sugar, flour, mayonnaise, warm water, egg, cocoa, baking soda, and vanilla until smooth and glossy, about 3 minutes, stopping to scrape down the sides of the bowl with a rubber spatula as needed. Divide the batter evenly between the prepared pans and smooth the tops with the spatula.

Bake the cake layers until a wooden toothpick inserted in the center of each cake comes out clean, about 35 minutes. Let the cakes cool in the pans on wire racks for 10 minutes. Run a thin-bladed knife around the inside of each pan to release the cake sides. Invert a rack on top of 1 cake, invert the cake and rack together, and then carefully lift off the pan. Peel off and discard the waxed paper. Turn the cake layer right side up. Repeat with the second cake layer. Let cool completely.

To make the Frosting, in a saucepan over medium heat, combine the evaporated milk, sugar, butter, egg yolks, vanilla, and salt and heat, stirring constantly, until the mixture comes to a boil. Continue cooking, stirring constantly, until the mixture is a shade darker with very thick bubbles, about 8 minutes more. Pour into a heatproof bowl and stir in the coconut and pecans. At this point, the frosting will look thin. Refrigerate, uncovered, until the frosting thickens enough for spreading, about 30 minutes.

Place the cookies in a lock-top plastic bag. Using a rolling pin, smash the cookies into coarse crumbs. Working in batches, transfer the coarse cookie crumbs to a food processor fitted with the metal chopping blade and pulse until reduced to fine crumbs. You should have about 1¼ cups. Pour the crumbs onto a rimmed baking sheet.

To assemble the cake, spoon a dollop of frosting in the center of an 8-inch cardboard round (or use the base of a tart or springform pan). Place a cake layer, top side down, on the round. Using an offset spatula, spread 1½ cups of the cooled frosting over the layer to the edges. Place the second layer, top side up, on the frosting and press gently to secure the 2 layers. Spread the remaining frosting on the top and sides of the cake. Don't worry if the cake isn't perfectly smooth and even. The crumbs will disguise any flaws.

Use one hand to hold the cake over the baking sheet of cookie crumbs. Use your other hand to press the crumbs onto the sides of the cake, letting any crumbs that don't stick fall back onto the baking sheet. Do not coat the top of the cake with crumbs. Refrigerate for about 30 minutes to set the frosting and the crumb coating, and then serve. (The cake can be made up to 1 day ahead, loosely covered with plastic wrap, and refrigerated. Remove the cake from the refrigerator at least 1 hour before serving.)

CHEF'S NOTE: *To toast pecans, spread them on a rimmed baking sheet and place in a preheated 350°F oven. Toast the nuts, stirring occasionally, until they are fragrant and have darkened, about 12 minutes. Pour onto a plate and let cool completely before chopping. This technique also works for macadamia nuts.*

HONEY AND VANILLA CHEESECAKE

This recipe is a house favorite. The straightforward flavors of honey and vanilla offset each other for a wonderfully rich and flavorful experience. A food processor is the best choice here because an electric mixer can beat too much air into the batter, which will cause the cheesecake to crack during cooling. And do search out vanilla bean paste, as it adds lots of true vanilla flavor. [CHEF ROB GIBBS]

Serves 10 to 12

PECAN CRUST

½ cup (1 stick) unsalted butter, melted and cooled

1½ cups graham cracker crumbs (about 18 crackers)

½ cup (2 ounces) chopped toasted pecans (see Chef's Note, page 207)

2 tablespoons sugar

FILLING

3 packages (8 ounces each) cream cheese, at room temperature

½ cup sugar

½ cup sour cream, at room temperature

¼ cup honey, preferably clover, plus more for serving

4 large eggs

2 large egg yolks

2 teaspoons vanilla bean paste (see Chef's Note, page 210)

Preheat the oven to 350°F. Butter the bottom and sides of a 10-inch round springform pan with 1½ teaspoons of the melted butter. Line the bottom with parchment paper. Brush the parchment with 1½ teaspoons of the butter.

To make the Pecan Crust, in a bowl, stir together the cracker crumbs, pecans, and sugar. Add the remaining 7 tablespoons butter and stir until the mixture is evenly moistened. Transfer the mixture to the prepared pan and press firmly and evenly onto the bottom.

Bake the crust until it is crisp and set, about 6 minutes. Transfer to a wire rack. Leave the oven on.

To make the Filling, in a food processor fitted with the metal chopping blade, process the cream cheese until lighter in texture. Add the sugar, sour cream, honey, eggs, egg yolks, and vanilla paste and process until thoroughly combined and smooth, stopping to scrape down the sides of the bowl as needed with a rubber spatula. Carefully pour the filling into the crust and smooth the top with a rubber spatula. Rap the pan against the counter to expel any trapped air.

Bake the cheesecake for 15 minutes. Reduce the oven temperature to 325°F and bake until the edges are puffed and barely beginning to brown, about 35 minutes. The center of the cake may look unset, but it will be firm when the cake has cooled. Turn off the oven and leave the oven door ajar. Let the cheesecake stand in the oven for 45 minutes. Transfer to a wire rack and let cool completely.

continued >

Run a thin-bladed knife around the inside of the pan to release the sides of the cheesecake, and then remove the sides of the pan. Cover with plastic wrap and refrigerate until chilled, at least 4 hours. (The cheesecake can be made up to 3 days ahead, covered, and refrigerated.)

Cut into wedges, dipping the knife blade into hot water before each cut and wiping it clean after each cut. Serve chilled and drizzle with a little honey, if desired.

CHEF'S NOTE: *Vanilla bean paste distributes tiny vanilla seeds throughout a dessert to give it a professional look. It saves the cook some time because you don't have to scrape vanilla seeds out of the split pods. Look for it at specialty-food stores, through mail-order sources, and at well-stocked supermarkets. If you prefer to use vanilla beans, substitute the seeds from 1 vanilla bean and ¼ teaspoon pure vanilla extract for each teaspoon of paste, though the paste has a somewhat stronger flavor.*

CHOCOLATE CHIP ICE CREAM SANDWICHES

I often make ice cream sandwiches when my son has his friends over, and I can attest to the fact that everyone in the family loves this recipe. It is fun to let the kids stuff the cookies themselves—just be prepared for an adult-sized cleanup. Nothing beats homemade ice cream, but you can use 1½ pints store-bought if you prefer. [MICHAEL THOMS]

Makes 6 sandwiches

CHOCOLATE CHIP ICE CREAM

⅔ cup (4 ounces) semisweet chocolate morsels

2 cups heavy (whipping) cream

½ cup granulated sugar

4 large egg yolks

1 teaspoon pure vanilla extract

DOUBLE CHOCOLATE CHIP COOKIES

1 cup (2 sticks) unsalted butter, at room temperature, plus more for the pans

2 cups all-purpose flour

⅓ cup unsweetened natural cocoa powder (not Dutch processed)

1 teaspoon baking soda

1 teaspoon salt

1 cup granulated sugar

1 cup firmly packed light brown sugar

2 large eggs, at room temperature

1 teaspoon pure vanilla extract

3 cups (18 ounces) semisweet chocolate morsels

Make the ice cream 1 day before serving to allow it to harden. Bring 1 inch of water to a simmer in the bottom of a double boiler or in a saucepan. Place the chocolate morsels in the top of the double boiler or in a heatproof bowl and place over (not touching) the water. Heat, stirring occasionally, until the chocolate is melted and smooth. Remove from the heat and set aside.

Fill a large bowl with a mixture of ice cubes and water to use for cooling the custard and set aside. In a saucepan over medium heat, bring the cream to a simmer. Meanwhile, in a small bowl, whisk together the sugar and egg yolks until the mixture is pale and thickened. Gradually whisk in ½ cup of the hot cream. Whisk the combined mixtures back into the saucepan over medium-low heat. Cook, stirring constantly with a wooden spatula (be sure to scrape the bottom and sides of the saucepan), until the custard is thick enough to coat the back of a spoon and an instant-read thermometer inserted into it reads 180°F. Strain the custard through a fine-mesh sieve set over a heatproof bowl.

Swirl the melted chocolate and vanilla into the custard. Cover with plastic wrap pressed directly on the surface, and pierce the plastic with a few slits to allow steam to escape. Place the bowl in the ice-water bath. Let stand, adding more ice to the water as needed to keep the water ice-cold, until the custard is chilled, about 1 hour.

Pour the custard into the canister of an ice cream maker and freeze according to the manufacturer's instructions. Transfer to an airtight container and freeze until firm, about 24 hours. (The ice cream can be made up to 2 days ahead.)

To make the Double Chocolate Chip Cookies, position 1 rack in the upper third of the oven and a second rack in the center of the oven, and preheat the oven to 375°F. Butter 2 baking sheets.

In a bowl, sift together the flour, cocoa, baking soda, and salt. In a bowl, using an electric mixer on high speed, beat together the butter and granulated and brown sugars until light and fluffy, about 3 minutes, stopping to scrape down the sides of the bowls as needed with a rubber spatula. Beat in the eggs, one at a time, beating well after each addition. Beat in the vanilla. Using a wooden spoon, stir in the flour in 2 equal additions, and then mix in the chocolate morsels until evenly distributed.

continued >

Using about ⅓ cup for each cookie, roll the dough between your palms into a ball about 2½ inches in diameter and place the balls on the prepared baking sheets, spacing them about 3 inches apart. You should have 12 balls in all. Gently flatten each ball into a disk about ½ inch thick.

Bake the cookies for 6 minutes. Switch the baking sheets between the racks and rotate them 180 degrees and continue baking until the edges are golden brown, about 6 minutes more. Let the cookies cool on the baking sheets on wire racks for 3 minutes, and then transfer them to the racks. Let cool completely.

To assemble, allow the ice cream to soften slightly at room temperature. Turn 6 cookies bottom side up on a work surface. Using an ice cream scoop, place about ⅔ cup ice cream on each cookie. Top with the remaining 6 cookies, bottom side down, and press gently to spread the ice cream to the edge. Serve immediately. (The cookie sandwiches can be prepared up to 8 hours ahead. Wrap each sandwich airtight in plastic wrap and freeze.)

MILK CHOCOLATE CHEESECAKE

I used to offer this cheesecake in a restaurant that included Hollywood producers as backers. While the dessert is somewhat traditional in approach, it has an understated decadence that ensures it is different enough that it will always be noticed. Sound like any movies you've seen lately? Make the cake the day before serving so it has plenty of time to chill. [CHEF MICHAEL NORTHERN]

Serves 10 to 12

COOKIE CRUST

½ cup (1 stick) unsalted butter, melted, plus more for the pan

20 cream-filled chocolate sandwich cookies

¼ teaspoon fine sea salt

FILLING

12 ounces high-quality milk chocolate, coarsely chopped

1 cup heavy (whipping) cream

¼ cup unsweetened natural cocoa powder (not Dutch processed)

3 packages (8 ounces each) cream cheese, at room temperature

5 large eggs, lightly beaten

1½ cups firmly packed light brown sugar

2 teaspoons pure vanilla extract

To make the Cookie Crust, preheat the oven to 375°F. Butter the bottom and sides of a 10-inch round springform pan with 1½ teaspoons of the melted butter. Line the bottom with parchment paper. Brush the parchment with 1½ teaspoons of the butter.

Place the cookies in a lock-top plastic bag. Using a rolling pin, smash the cookies into coarse crumbs. Working in batches, transfer the coarse cookie crumbs to a food processor fitted with the metal chopping blade and pulse until reduced to fine crumbs. You should have 2 cups.

In a bowl, stir together the cookie crumbs and salt. Add the remaining 7 tablespoons butter and stir until the mixture is evenly moistened. Transfer the crumb mixture to the prepared pan and press firmly and evenly onto the bottom and halfway up the sides.

Bake the crust until it is crisp and set, about 8 minutes. Transfer to a wire rack. Reduce the oven temperature to 325°F.

To make the Filling, bring 1 inch of water to a simmer in the bottom of a double boiler or in a saucepan. Combine the chocolate, cream, and cocoa in the top of the double boiler or in a heatproof bowl and place over (not touching) the water. Heat, stirring occasionally, until the chocolate melts and the mixture is smooth. Remove from the heat and let stand, stirring often, until the mixture is tepid.

In a food processor fitted with the metal chopping blade, process the cream cheese until lighter in texture. Add the eggs, sugar, and vanilla and process until thoroughly combined and smooth, stopping to scrape down the sides of the bowl as needed with a rubber spatula. With the machine running, gradually add the chocolate mixture in a thin, steady stream. Process until evenly colored, again stopping to scrape down the sides of the bowl as needed. Carefully pour the batter into the crust and smooth the top with the spatula. Rap the pan against the counter to expel any trapped air.

Bake the cheesecake until the edges are puffed and have pulled away from the pan slightly and the center is barely set, about 1 hour. Turn off the oven and leave the oven door ajar. Let the cheesecake stand in the oven for 1 hour. Transfer to a wire rack and let cool completely. Cover the cheesecake with plastic wrap and refrigerate until well chilled, at least 6 hours or up to overnight.

To serve, run a thin-bladed knife around the inside of the pan to release the sides of the cheesecake, and then remove the sides of the pan. Slip a long, thin-bladed, sharp knife between the crust and parchment paper to separate them, and then carefully slide the paper out from under the cheesecake. Cut the cake into wedges, dipping the knife blade into hot water before each cut and wiping it clean after each cut. Serve chilled.

CHEF'S NOTE: *There are a few ways to melt chocolate, including in a microwave, but for the most control, I prefer to heat the chopped chocolate gently over barely simmering water. Place the chocolate in the top part of a double boiler or in a stainless-steel or other heatproof bowl. Bring about 1 inch of water to a bare simmer in the bottom of the double boiler or in a saucepan. Nest the bowl over (not touching) the simmering water and let the chocolate melt, stirring it occasionally with a rubber spatula. Gentle heat is particularly important when melting milk and white chocolates because they are more delicate than dark chocolate and may scorch if overheated.*

VANILLA BEAN POUND CAKE

This is a tweaked recipe of my wife's grandmother, Mamma Mary. Her pound cake is always the highlight of our family gatherings, and she assures everyone that the thinner you slice it, the better it tastes. On the other hand, I can't help but cut big slices and serve them with fresh Georgia peaches. (And if you are of a mind to grill the peaches, so much the better.) [CHEF JONATHAN ROHLAND]

Serves 12

1½ cups (3 sticks) unsalted butter, at room temperature, plus more for the pan

3 cups sifted all-purpose flour, plus more for the pan

3 vanilla beans, preferably Tahitian, split lengthwise

1 cup buttermilk

1 teaspoon baking powder

½ teaspoon fine sea salt

3 cups sugar

6 large eggs, at room temperature

Preheat the oven to 325°F. Butter a 10-inch tube pan. Dust the pan with flour, tapping out the excess.

Place the butter in a large bowl. Using the tip of a small knife, scrape the seeds from the vanilla pods into the bowl. Set aside.

In a saucepan over medium-low heat, combine the buttermilk and vanilla pods and heat just to a simmer. Remove from the heat and let cool completely, then remove and discard the pods.

In a bowl, sift together the flour, baking powder, and salt. Add the sugar to the butter and vanilla seeds. Using an electric mixer on high speed, beat the butter mixture until light and fluffy, about 3 minutes, stopping to scrape down the sides of the bowl as needed with a rubber spatula. Add the eggs, two at a time, beating well after each addition. On low speed, add the flour mixture in 3 equal additions alternately with the buttermilk in 2 equal additions, beginning and ending with the flour mixture and beating just until incorporated after each addition. Do not overbeat, and stop to scrape down the sides of the bowl as needed. Using the spatula, scrape the batter into the prepared pan and smooth the top.

Bake the cake, rotating the pan 180 degrees after 30 minutes to ensure it browns evenly, until a wooden toothpick inserted in the center comes out clean, 1 to 1¼ hours. Let cool in the pan on a wire rack for 15 minutes. Run a thin-bladed knife around the inside of the pan and around the tube to release the cake. Invert a rack on top of the cake, invert the cake and rack together, and then carefully lift off the pan. Turn the cake right side up to cool.

Serve the cake warm or at room temperature.

CHEF'S NOTE: *Bourbon vanilla beans have nothing to do with whiskey. Vanilla can only be grown in tropical regions, and the island of Reúnion (formerly called Bourbon) is one place where the vanilla orchid is grown. Vanilla is also harvested in Madagascar, another island whose name is often on vanilla labels. The same vanilla species is grown in Mexico as on Reúnion and Madagascar, so Mexican vanilla is similar in flavor, though each remains distinctive because of soil and climate conditions where it is grown. Vanilla beans from Tahiti are a different species, however. They are plump and highly fragrant with fruity aromas, but they contain less vanillin (the natural compound that gives vanilla beans their flavor), so their vanilla flavor is less pronounced, which some cooks prefer. What you use is a matter of personal taste—and what you can find at the store.*

Index

Acknowledgments

This book would never have been possible without the inspired efforts of the Nordstrom chef contributors. They all took valuable time out of their busy work and home schedules to make this extraordinary collection of recipes possible. These seasoned professionals went above and beyond the call of duty to help create the fabric and flavor of this book: John Barron, Keith Breedlove, Tony Colabelli, Jenny-Lynn Fischer, Rob Gibbs, Cory Goodman, Kimberly Hazard, Alyssa Kasparek, David Kim, Nawai Kekoolani, Richard Ladd, Michael Lyle, Jonah Merrell, Jaime Montilla, Joe Noonan, Michael Palesh, Jonathan Rohland, Vincent Rossetti, Eric Salzer, Richard Silva, Michael Thoms, Richard Venzor, Daniel Wood, and Faris Zoma.

I was blessed with the experience, wisdom, and guidance of Rick Rodgers during the creation and writing of this book. Rick generously drew on his culinary knowledge, gained by authoring over sixty cookbooks during his busy, productive career. He receives a culinary Purple Heart for all of his efforts and contributions toward transforming these recipes from rough form into polished, trustworthy copy.

An extremely talented duo of cooking professionals tested, evaluated, and improved each and every recipe. I have great appreciation for all of the time, energy, support, and insight provided by chef Richard Silva and chef Daniel Wood. Thank you for your hard work in seeing this book through to its conclusion.

I would never attempt to write a book without the behind-the-scenes support and exceptional talents of Laurel Ewing, who provided constant nurturing, insight, and administrative guidance. Thank you, Laurel, for helping to bring this book to reality.

It was a pleasure to work with photographer Noel Barnhurst and his entire team, who took our recipes and made them even more enticing, encouraging readers to make them for themselves and their friends and family. Special recognition is due food stylist George Dolese, a master of making good food look great.

To the staff at Chronicle Books, including Pamela Geismar, Laurel Leigh, and Sharon Silva, my many thanks for their patience and expert guidance throughout the evolution of this project. Designer Gretchen Scoble has once again worked with the team to create the appetizing visual look of the book, and, once again, she has my sincere gratitude.

Finally, a heartfelt thanks to my friends and family, who provided an environment of inspiration, care, and nurturing that made this effort a joy.

—Michael Northern